Leo Tolstoy

Patriotism and Christianity

Leo Tolstoy

Patriotism and Christianity

ISBN/EAN: 9783337309831

Printed in Europe, USA, Canada, Australia, Japan

Cover: Foto ©Thomas Meinert / pixelio.de

More available books at **www.hansebooks.com**

PATRIOTISM

AND

CHRISTIANITY

TO WHICH IS APPENDED

"A REPLY TO CRITICISMS" OF THE WORK

AND

"PATRIOTISM, OR PEACE?"

A Letter called forth by the Venezuelan dispute between England and the United States...

BY

COUNT LEO TOLSTOY

With a Note to English Readers by
JOHN C. KENWORTHY.

LONDON
WALTER SCOTT, LTD., PATERNOSTER SQUARE
1896

NOTE TO ENGLISH READERS.

IN this remarkable work by Leo Tolstoy, which powerfully aroused European attention a year ago, the principle of "non-resistance," which is so often, by opponents, made to take a *doctrinaire*, or even absurd complexion, is seen in drastic application to the huge militarism under which the world groans. As reasonable people, following Tolstoy, we must ask: "What other principle of conduct than this, can possibly remove the incubus?"

To us, in England, the unusual contentions of this work may not seem so startling as to those who live under a system of compulsory military service. But a little thought reminds us that we also maintain hundreds of thousands of fighting-men, and that in paying taxes for government purposes, we are responsible for the appearance, upon the sea and in the field, of those whom Tolstoy might call "licensed murderers." So that the obligation of conscience raised by this book is equally binding upon all, whether Russian or English, French or American.

JOHN C. KENWORTHY.

March, 1896.

PATRIOTISM AND CHRISTIANITY.

THE Franco-Russian festivities which took place in October 1894 in France made me, and others, no doubt, as well, first amused, then astonished, then indignant—feelings which I wished to express in a short article.

But while studying further the chief causes of what had occurred, I arrived at the reflections which I here offer to the reader.

I.

The Russian and French peoples have lived for many centuries with a knowledge of each other—entering sometimes into friendly, more often, unfortunately, into very unfriendly, relations at the instigation of their respective Governments—when suddenly, because two years ago a French squadron came to Cronstadt, and its officers having landed, eaten much, and drunk a variety of wine in various places, heard and made many false and foolish speeches ; and because last year a Russian squadron arrived at Toulon, and its officers having gone to Paris and there eaten and drunk copiously, heard and made a still greater number of silly and untruthful speeches, it came to pass that not only those who ate, drank and spoke, but every one who was present, and even those who merely heard or read in the papers of these proceedings—all these millions of French and Russians—imagined suddenly that in some especial fashion they were enamoured of each other; that is, that all the French love all the Russians, and all the Russians all the French.

These sentiments were expressed in France in the most unheard-of ways by what took place in October.

The following description of these proceedings appeared in the *Village Review*, a paper which collects its information from the daily Press:—

"When the French and Russian squadrons met they greeted each other with salvos of artillery, and with ardent and enthusiastic cries of 'Hurrah!' 'Long live Russia!' 'Long live France!'

"To all this uproar the naval bands (there were orchestras also on most of the hired steamboats) contributed, the Russian playing 'God save the Tsar,' and the French the 'Marseillaise,' the public upon the steamboats waving their hats, flags, handkerchiefs and nosegays. Many barges were loaded entirely with men and women of the working class with their children, waving nosegays and shouting 'Long live Russia!' with all their might. Our sailors in view of such national enthusiasm, could not restrain their tears.

"In the harbour all the French men-of-war present were ranged in two divisions, and our fleet passed between them, the admiral's vessel leading. A splendid moment was approaching.

"A salute of fifteen guns was fired from the Russian flagship in honour of the French fleet, and the French flagship replied with thirty. The Russian National Hymn pealed from the French lines: French sailors mounted their masts and rigging: vociferations of welcome poured uninterruptedly from both fleets, and from the surrounding vessels. The sailors waved their caps, the spectators their hats and handkerchiefs in honour of the dear guests. From all sides, sea and shore, thundered the universal shout, 'Long live Russia!' 'Long live France!'

"According to the custom in naval visits, Admiral Avellan and the officers of his staff came on shore in order to pay their respects to the local authorities.

"At the landing stage they were met by the French naval staff and the senior officials of the port of Toulon.

"Friendly greetings followed, accompanied by the thunder of artillery and the pealing of bells. The naval band played the Russian National Hymn, 'God save the Tsar,' which was received with a roar from the spectators of 'Long live the Tsar!' 'Long live Russia!'

"The shouting swelled into one mighty din, which drowned the music and even the cannonade. Those present declare that the enthusiasm of the huge crowd of people attained at that moment its utmost height, and that it would be impossible to express in words the feelings which overflowed the hearts of all upon the scene.

"Admiral Avellan, with uncovered head, and accompanied by the French and Russian officers, then drove to the naval administration buildings, where he was received by the French Minister of Marine.

"In welcoming the Admiral, the Minister said, ' Constadt and Toulon have severally witnessed the sympathy which exists between the French and Russian peoples. Everywhere you will be received as the most welcome of friends.

"Our Government and all France greet you and your comrades on your arrival as the representatives of a great and honourable nation.

"The admiral replied that he was unable to find language to express his feelings. ' The Russian fleet, and all Russia,' he said, ' will be grateful to you for this reception.'

"After some further speeches, the Admiral again, in taking leave of the Minister, thanked him for his reception, and added, ' I cannot leave you without pronouncing the words which are written in the hearts of every Russian : ' Long live France !' "

Such was the reception at Toulon. In Paris the welcome and the festivities were still more extraordinary.

The following is a description taken from the papers of the reception in Paris :—

"All eyes are directed towards the Boulevard des Italiens, whence the Russian sailors are expected to emerge. At length, far away, the murmur of a whole hurricane of shouts and cheers is heard. The hurricane approaches. The crowd surges in the Place. The police press forward to clear the route to the Cercle . Militaire, but the task is not an easy one. The spectators lunge forward irrepressibly. . . . At last the head of the cortège appears, and the Place is deluged at once with an astounding shout of ' Long live Russia !' ' Long live the Russians !'

"All heads are uncovered; spectators fill the windows and balconies, they even cover the house-tops ; waving] handkerchiefs, flags, hats, cheering enthusiastically and flinging clouds of tricolour cockades from the upper windows. A sea of handkerchiefs, hats, and flags waves over the heads of the crowd below, shouting frantically ' Long live Russia ! ' from a hundred thousand throats surging to and fro, and making wild efforts to catch a glimpse of the dear guests, craning their necks, hither and thither, and trying in every possible way to express its enthusiasm."

Another correspondent writes that the rapture of the crowd was like a delirium. A Russian journalist who was in Paris at the time thus describes the entry of the Russian officers ;—

" It may truthfully be said that this event is of universal importance, astounding, sufficiently touching to produce tears, an elevating influence on the soul, making it throb with *that love which sees in men brothers, which hates blood, and violence, and the snatching of children from a beloved mother.* I have been in a kind of torpor for the last few hours. It seemed almost overpoweringly strange to stand in the terminus of the Lyons Railway amid the representatives of the French Government in their uniforms embroidered with gold, amongst the municipal authorities in full dress, and to hear cries of ' Long live Russia !' ' Long live the Tsar ! ' and our national anthem played again and again.

" Where am I ? I reflected. What has happened ? What magic current has floated all these feelings, these aspirations into one stream ? Is not this the sensible presence of the God of love and of fraternity ; the presence of the loftiest ideal descending in his supremest moments upon man ?

" My soul is so full of something beautiful, pure and elevated that my pen is unable to express it. Words are weak in comparison with what I saw and felt. It was not rapture, the word is too commonplace ; it was better than rapture. More picturesque, deeper, happier, more various. It is impossible to describe what took place at the Cercle Militaire when Admiral Avellan appeared on the balcony of the second story. Words here are of no avail. During the ' Te Deum,' while the choir in the church was singing, ' O Lord save Thy people,' through the open door was blown the triumphal strains of the ' Marseillaise,' played by the brass bands in the street.

" It produced an astounding, an inexpressible impression."

II.

On arriving in France the Russian sailors passed during a fortnight, from one festivity to another, and during or after each they ate, drank, and made speeches. Information as to where and what they ate and drank on Wednesday, and where and what on Friday, and what they said on these occasions was purveyed by telegraph to the whole of Russia.

The moment one of the Russian commanders had drunk to the health of France, it became known to the whole world; and the instant the Russian Admiral had said " I drink to beautiful France," his effusion was transmitted round the globe. More, for such was the solicitude of the papers that they commemorated not merely the toasts, but the dishes, not even omitting the hors-d'œuvres or zakouskas which were consumed.

For instance, the following menu was published, with the comment that the dinner it represented was a work of art.

Consommé de volailles; petits pâtés.
Mousse de homard parisienne.
Noisette de bœuf à la béarnaise.
Faisans à la Périgueux.
Casseroles de truffes au champagne.
Chaudfroid de volailles à la Toulouse.
Salade russe.
Croûte de fruits toulonnaise.
Parfaits à l'ananas.
Dessert.

In a second number was the following :—

Potage livonien et Saint-Germain.
Zéphyrs Nantua.
Esturgeon braisé moldave.
Sel de daguet grand veneur.

And a following issue gave a third menu followed by a minute description of the wine list—such vodka, such old Burgandy, Grand Moët, etc.

In an English journal the amount of intoxicating liquor drunk during the festivities was given. The quantity mentioned was so enormous that one hardly believes it would have been possible that all the drunkards in France and Russia could account for so much in so short a time.

The speeches made were also published, but the menus were more varied than the speeches. The latter, without exception, always consisted of the same words in different combinations. The meaning of these words was always the same—We love each other tenderly, and are enraptured to be so tenderly in love. Our aim is not war, not a " *revanche*," not the recovery of the lost provinces ;

our aim is only *peace*, the furtherance of *peace*, the security of *peace*, the tranquility and *peace* of Europe.

Long live the Russian Emperor and Empress! We love them, and we love *peace*. Long live the President of the Republic and his wife! We love them and we love *peace*. Long live France, Russia, their fleets and their armies! We love the army, and *peace*, and the commander of the Russian fleet.

The speeches concluded for the most part, like some popular ditty, with a refrain, " Toulon-Cronstadt," or " Cronstadt-Toulon." And the reiteration of the names of these places, where so many different dishes had been eaten and so many kinds of wine drunk, were pronounced as words which should stimulate the representatives of either nation to the noblest deeds—as words which require no commentary, being full of deep meaning in themselves.

" We love each other ; we love peace. Cronstadt-Toulon ! " What more can be said, especially to the sound of glorious music, performing at one and the same time two national anthems—one glorifying the Tsar and praying for him all possible good fortune, the other cursing all Tsars and promising them destruction ?

Those who expressed their sentiments of love especially well on these occasions received orders and rewards. Others, either for the same reason or from the exuberance of the feelings of the givers, were presented with articles of the strangest and most unexpected kind. A French Province presented to the Tsar a book in which, it seems, nothing was written—or, at least, nothing of any concern—and the Russian admiral received an aluminium plough covered with flowers, and many other trifles equally astonishing.

Moreover, all these strange acts were accompanied by yet stranger religious ceremonies and society services to which one might suppose Frenchmen have long since become unaccustomed.

Since the time of the Concordat scarcely so many prayers can have been pronounced as during this short period. All the French suddenly became very religious, and carefully deposited in the rooms of the Russian mariners the very images which a short time previously they had as carefully removed from their schools as harmful tools of superstition, and they said prayers incessantly. The Cardinals and Bishops everywhere enjoined devotions, and themselves pronounced some of the strangest. Thus a bishop at Toulon, at the launch of a certain ironclad, addressed the God of

Peace, letting it, however, at the same time be felt that he could communicate as readily, if the necessity arose, with the God of War.

" What its destination may be," said the bishop, alluding to the vessel, " God only knows. Will it vomit death from its dreadful bowels? We do not know. But if, having to-day pleaded with the God of Peace we may hereafter have to call upon the God of War, we may be sure that it will advance against the foe in rank with the powerful men-of-war whose crews have to-day entered into so near and fraternal union with us. But let this contingency be forgotten, and let the present festival leave none but peaceful memories, like those that the Grand Duke Constantine—(Constantine Nikolaevitch visited Toulon in 1857)—may cherish, and may the friendship of France and Russia constitute of these two nations the guardians of peace !"

At the same time tens of thousands of telegrams flew from Russia to France and from France to Russia.

French women greeted Russian women, and Russian women tendered their thanks to the French. A troupe of Russian actors greeted the French actors ; the French actors replied that they had laid deep in their hearts the greetings of their Russian comrades.

The Russian law students of some Russian town or other expressed their rapture to the French nation. General So-and-so thanked Madame This-and-that ; Madame This-and-that assured General So-and-so of the ardour of her sentiments towards the Russian nation. Russian children wrote greetings in verse to French children ; the French children replied in verse and prose. The Russian Minister of Education assured the French Minister of Education of the sudden amity towards France of all the children, clerks and scientists in his department. The members of the Society for the Prevention of Cruelty to Animals expressed their warm attachment towards the French. The Municipality of Kazan did the same.

The Canon of Arrare conveyed to the most reverend Dean of the Court Clergy the assurance that a deep affection towards Russia, his Imperial Majesty the Emperor, and all the Imperial Family, exists in the hearts of all the French Cardinals and Bishops, and that the French and Russian clergy profess almost a similar faith, and alike worship the Holy Virgin. To this the most reverend dean replied that the prayers of the French clergy for the Imperial Family were joyously echoed by all the Russian people, lovingly attached to the Tsar, and that as the Russian nation also worships the Holy Virgin, France may count upon it in life and death. The same kind of messages were sent by various generals, telegraph clerks and shopkeepers.

Everyone sent congratulations to everyone else, and thanked somebody for something.

The excitement was so great that some extraordinary things were done ; and yet no one remarked their strangeness, but on the contrary every one approved of them, was charmed with them, and as if afraid of being left behind, made haste to accomplish something of a similar kind in order not to be outdone by the rest.

If at times protests, pronounced or even written and printed, against this madness made their appearance, proving its un-reasonableness they were either hushed up or concealed.*

---

* Thus I am aware of the following protest which was made by Russian students and sent to Paris, but not accepted by any of the papers :—

"A OPEN LETTER TO FRENCH STUDENTS.

"A short time back a small body of Moscow law students, headed by its inspector, was bold enough to speak in the person of the university concerning the Toulon festivities.

"We, the representatives of the united students of various provinces, protest most emphatically against the pretensions of this body, and in substance against the interchange of greetings which has taken place between it and the French students. We likewise regard France with warm affection and deep respect, but we do so because we see in her a great nation which has always been in the past the introducter and announcer of the high ideals of freedom, equality, and brotherhood for all the world ; and first also in the bold attempts to incorporate these high ideals into life. The better part of Russian youth has always been prepared to acclaim France as the foremost fighter for a loftier future for mankind. But we do not regard such festivities as those of Constadt and Toulon as appropriate occasions for such greetings.

"On the contrary, these receptions represent a sad, but, we hope, a temporary condition—the treason of France to its great historical role of the past. The country which at one time invited all the world to break the chains of despotism, and offered its fraternal aid to any nation which might revolt in order to obtain its freedom, now burns incense before the Russian Government, which systematically impedes the normal organic growth of a people's life, and relentlessly crushes without consideration every aspiration of Russian society towards light, freedom and independence. The Toulon manifestations are one act of a drama in the antagonism between France and Germany created by Bismarck and Napoleon III.

' This antagonism keeps all Europe under arms, and gives the deciding vote in

Not to mention the millions of working days spent in these festivities, the widespread drunkenness of all who took part in them involving even those in command ; not to speak of the senselessness of the speeches which were made, the most insane and ruthless deeds were committed, and no one paid them any attention.

For instance, several score of people were crushed to death, and no one found it necessary to record the fact.

One correspondent wrote that he had been informed at a ball that there was scarcely a woman in Paris who would not have been ready to forget her duties to satisfy the desire of any of the Russian sailors.

And all this passed unremarked as something quite in the order of things. There were also cases of unmistakable insanity brought about by the excitement.

Thus one woman, having put on a dress composed of the colours of the Franco Russian flags, awaited on a bridge the arrival of the Russian sailors, and threw herself into the river, and was drowned.

In general the women on all these occasions played a more prominent part than, and even directed the men. Besides the throwing of flowers and various little ribbons and the presenting of gifts and addresses, the French women in the streets threw themselves into the arms of the Russian sailors and kissed them.

Some women brought their children, for some reason or other to be kissed, and when the Russian sailors had granted this request, all present were transported with joy and shed tears.

This strange excitement was so contagious that, as one correspondent relates, a Russian sailor who appeared to be in perfect

---

European affairs to Russian despotism, which has ever been the support of all that is arbitrary and absolute against freedom, and of tyrants against the tyrannised.

"A sense of pain for our country, of regret at the blindness of so great a portion of French society, these are the feelings called forth in us by these festivities.

"We are persuaded that the younger generation in France is not allured by national Chauvinism, and that, ready to struggle for that better social condition towards which humanity is advancing, it will know how to interpret present events, and what attitude to adopt towards them. We hope that our determined protest will find an echo in the hearts of the French youth.

"(Signed), The United Council of Twenty-four Federate Societies of Moscow Students."

health, after having witnessed these exciting scenes for a fortnight jumped overboard in the middle of the day, and swam about crying "Long live France." When pulled out of the water, and questioned as to his conduct he replied that he had vowed to swim round his ship in honour of France.

Thus the unthwarted excitement grew and grew, like a ball of snow, and finally attained sach dimensions that not alone those on the spot, or merely nervous predisposed persons, but strong healthy men were affected by the general strain and were betrayed into an abnormal condition of mind.

I remember even that whilst reading distractedly a description of these festivities, I was suddenly overcome by strong emotion, and was almost on the verge of tears, having to check with an effort this expression of my feelings.

III.

A professor of psychology, Sikorsky by name, has described in the *Kief University Review* a psychical epidemic of, as he calls it, Malevanchina, which he studied in the district of Vassilkoff. The feature of this epidemic, according to M. Sikorsky, was the conviction in the minds of the peasants of certain villages, under the influence of their leader, Malevani, that the end of the world was at hand; in consequence of which they changed their mood of life, began to dispose of their property, to adorn their clothing, eat and drink of the best, and cease to work. The professor considered this condition abnormal. He says, "Their remarkable good humour often attained to a condition of exultation or euthanasia, and from no apparent cause. They were sentimental, polite to excess, talkative active in their movements, tears of happiness being readily summoned to their eyes, and disappearing without leaving a trace. They sold the necessaries of life in order to buy umbrellas, silk handkerchiefs, and similar articles which, however, they only wore as ornaments. They ate a great quantity of sweets. Their condition of mind was always joyous, they led a perfectly idle life, visiting each other and walking about together. . . . When chid for the insanity of their conduct and their idleness, they replied invariably with the same phrase:—'If it pleases me I will work; if it does not, why compel myself to?'"

The learned professor regards this condition as a well defined epidemic of morbid psychomachy, and in advising the Government to adopt measures to prevent its extension, concludes, "This Malevanchina is the cry of a sick population, a prayer for deliverance from drunkenness, and for improved educational and sanitary conditions."

But if Malevanchina is the cry of a sick population for deliverance from inebriety and from pernicious social conditions, what a terrible clamour of a sick people, and what a pertition for a rescue from the effects of wine and of a false social existance is that new disease which appeared in Paris with such fearful suddenness, infecting the greater part of the urban population of France, and almost the entire governmental, privileged, and civilised classes of Russia ?

But if we admit that danger exists in the psychical conditions of Malevanchina, and that the Government did well in following the professor's advice, by confining some the leaders of the Malevanchina in asylums and monasteries, and by banishing others into distant lands, how much more dangerous must we consider this new epidemic which has appeared in Toulon and Paris, and spread thence throughout Russia and France, and how much more needful is it that society—if the Government refuse to interfere—should take decisive measures to prevent the epidemic from spreading ?

The analogy between the two diseases is complete. The same remarkable good humour, passing into a vague and joyous ecstasy, the same sentimental, exaggerated politeness, loquacity, emotional weeping, without reason for its commencement or cessation, the same festal mood, the same promenading and paying calls, the same wearing of gorgeous clothes and fancy for choice food, the same misty and senseless speeches, the same indolence, singing and music, the same direction on the part of the women, tbe same clownish state of *attitudes passionées*, which M. Sikorsky observed, and which corresponds, as I understand it, with the various unnatural physical attitudes adopted by people during triumphal receptions, acclamations and after-dinner speeches.

The resemblance is absolute. The difference, an enormous one for the society in which these things take place, is merely that in one case a few scores of poor country folk have gone out of their mind, people who, living on their own small earnings, cannot do any violence to their neighbours and infect others only by personal and vocal communication of their condition, whereas in the other case millions of people have lost their reason who possess immense sums of money and means of violence—rifles, canon, fortresses, ironclads, mélinite, dynamite—and with, moreover, at their disposal, the most effective means for communicating their insanity: the post, telegraph, telephone, the entire Press, and every class of magazine, which prints the infection with the utmost haste, and distributes it throughout the world.

Another difference is that the former not only remain sober, but abstain from all intoxicating drinks, while the latter are in a constant state of semi-drunkenness which they do their best to foster.

Hence for the society in which such epidemics take place, the difference between that at Kief, when according to M. Sikorsky, no violence nor manslaughter was recorded, and that of Paris, where in one procession more than twenty women were crushed to death, is equivalent to that between the falling of a small piece of smouldering coal from the fireplace upon the floor and a fire which has already obtained possession of the floors and walls of the house.

At its worst the result of the outbreak at Kief will be that the peasants of a millionth part of Russia may spend the earnings of their own labour, and be unable to meet the Government taxes; but the outbreak at Paris and Toulon, which has affected people who have great power, immense sums of money, weapons of violence and means for the propagation of their insanity, may and must have a terrible conclusion.

IV.

One may listen with compassion to the mouthings of a feeble old and unarmed idiot in his cap and nightshirt, not contradicting and even humourously acquiescing with him ; but when a crowd of able bodied mad-men escape from confinement, armed to the teeth with knives, swords and revolvers, wild with excitement, waving their murderous weapons, one not only ceases to acquiesce, but one is unable to feel secure for an instant.

This case is very like that which has been evoked by the excitement of the Franco-Russian receptions which has taken possession of Russian and French society. Those who have succumbed to this psychical epidemic are the masters of the most terrible weapons of slaughter and destruction.

It is true that it was constantly proclaimed in every speech made to honour the toasts at these festivities, and in all the articles upon them, that the object of what was taking place was the establishment of peace. Even the partisans of war, the Russian correspondent previously cited amongst them, speak not of any hatred towards the conquerors of the lost provinces, but of a "love which somehow hates."

However, we are well aware of the cunning of mental sufferers, and we can realise that this constant repetition of a desire for peace, and silence as to the sentiments in every man's mind, is precisely a threat of the worst significance.

In his reply at the dinner at the Elysée the Russian Ambassador said—

"Before proposing a toast to which everyone will respond from the depths of his soul, not alone those within these walls, but all those, and with the same enthusiasm, whose hearts are at the present moment beating in unison with ours, far away or around us in great and beautiful France, as in Russia, permit me to offer an expression of the deepest gratitude for the welcome, addressed by you to the Admiral whom the Tsar deputed to return the Cronstadt visit. In the high position which you occupy your words express the full meaning of the glorious and pacific festivities which are now being celebrated with such remarkable unanimity, loyalty, and sincerity."

The same entirely baseless reference to peace may be found in the speech of the French President.

"The links of love which unite Russia and France," he said, "were strengthened two years ago by the touching manifestations of which our fleet was the object at Cronstadt, and are becoming every day more binding ; and the *honest* interchange of our friendly sentiments must inspire all those who have at heart the welfare of peace, security, and confidence," etc.

In both speeches the benefits of peace, and of peaceful festivities, are alluded to quite unexpectedly and without any occasion.

The same thing is observable in the interchange of telegrams between the Russian Emperor and the President of the Republic.

The Emperor telegraphs :—

"At the moment when the Russian fleet is leaving France it is my ardent wish to express to you how I am touched by, and grateful for, the chivalrous and splendid reception which my sailors have everywhere experienced on French soil. The expressions of warm sympathy which have been manifested once again with so much eloquence will add a fresh link to those which unite the two countries, and will I trust contribute to strengthen the general *peace* which is the object of our most constant efforts and desires."

The French President replies :—

"The telegram, for which I thank your Majesty, reached me when on the point of leaving Toulon to return to Paris.

"The magnificent fleet on which I had the great satisfaction of saluting the Russian pennant in French waters, the cordial and spontaneous reception which your brave sailors have everywhere received in France, prove gloriously once again the sincere sympathies which unite our two countries. They show at the same time a deep faith in the beneficent influence which may weld together two great nations devoted to the cause of *peace*."

Again, in both telegrams, without the slightest occasion, are allusions to peace which have nothing at all to do with the reception of the sailors.

There is no single speech nor article in which it is not said that the purpose of all these orgies is the peace of Europe. At a dinner given by the representatives of French literature, all breathe of peace. M. Zola, who, a short time previously, had written that war was inevitable, and even serviceable ; M. de Vogué, who more than once has stated the same in print, say, neither of them, a word as to war, but speak only of peace. The sessions of Parliament open with speeches upon the past festivities ; the speakers mention that such festivities are an assurance of peace to Europe.

It is as if a man should come into a peaceful company, and commence energetically to assure everyone present that he has not the least intention to knock out anyone's teeth, blacken their eyes, or break their arms, but has only the most peaceful ideas for passing the evening.

"But no one doubts it," one is inclined to say, "and if you really have such evil intentions, at least do not presume to mention them."

In many of the articles describing the festivities a naïve satisfaction is clearly expressed that no one during them alluded to what it was determined, by silent consent, to hide from everybody, and that only one incautious fellow, who was immediately removed by the police, voiced what all had in their minds by shouting, "Down with Germany!"

In the same way children are often so delighted at being able to conceal an escapade that their very high spirits betray them.

Why, indeed, be so glad that no one said anything about war, if the subject were not uppermost in our minds?

V.

No one is thinking of war; only a milliard is being spent upon preparations for it, and millions of men are under arms in France and Russia.

"But all this is done to insure peace. *Si vis pacem para bellum. L'empire c'est la paix. La République c'est la paix.*"

But if such be the case, why are the military advantages of a Franco-Russian alliance in the event of a war with Germany not only explained in every paper and magazine published for a so-called educated people, but also in the *Village Review*, a paper published for the people by the Russian Government? Why is it inculcated to this unfortunate people, cheated by its own Government, that "to be in friendly relations with France is profitable to Russia, because if, unexpectedly, the before-mentioned States (Germany, Austria, and Italy) made up their minds to declare war with Russia, then, though with God's help she might be able to withstand them by herself, and defeat even so considerable an alliance, the feat would not be an easy one, and great sacrifices and losses would be entailed by success."

And why in all French schools is history taught from the primer of M. Lavisse (twenty-first edition, 1889), in which the following is inserted:—

"Since the insurrection of the Commune France has had no further troubles. The day following the war she again resumed work. She paid Germany without difficulty the enormous war indemnity of five milliards.

"But France lost her military renown during the war of 1870. She has lost part of her territory. More than 15,000 inhabitants of our departments on the Upper Rhine, Lower Rhine, and Moselle who were good Frenchmen have been compelled to become Germans. But they are not resigned to their fate. They detest Germany; they continue to hope that they may once more be Frenchmen.

"But Germany appreciates its victory, and it is a great country, all the inhabitants of which sincerely love their fatherland, and

B

whose soldiers are brave and well disciplined.   In order to recover
from Germany what she took from us we must be good citizens and
soldiers.   It is to make you good soldiers that your teachers
instruct you in the history of France.

" The history of France proves that in our country the sons have
always avenged the disasters of their fathers.

" Frenchmen in the time of Charles VII. avenged the defeat of
their fathers at Crécy, at Poictiers, at Agincourt.

" It is for you, boys, being educated in our schools, to avenge
the defeat of your fathers at Sedan and at Metz.

" It is your duty—the great duty of your life.   You must ever
bear that in mind."

At the foot of the page is a series of questions upon the preced-
ing paragraph.   The questions are the following :—

" What has France lost by losing part of her territory ?"

" How many Frenchmen have become Germans by the loss of
this territory ?"

" Do these Frenchmen love Germany ?"

" What must we do to recover some day what Germany has
taken from us ?"

In addition to these there are certain " Reflections on Book VII,'
where it is said that " the children of France must not forget her
defeat of 1870 "; that they must bear on their hearts the burden
of this remembrance," but that " this memory must not discourage
them, on the contrary it must excite their courage."

So that if, in official speeches, peace is mentioned with such
emphasis, behind the scenes the lawfulness, profit and necessity of
war is incessantly urged upon the people, the rising generation,
and all Frenchmen and Russians.

" We do not think of war, we would only establish peace." One
feels inclined to inquire, " *Qui diable trompe-e-on ici ?*" if the question
were worth asking, and it were not too evident who was the
unhappy deluded one.

The deceived are always the same eternally deluded, foolish
working-folk, those who, with horny hands, make all these ships,
forts, arsenals, barracks, cannon, steamers, harbours, piers,
palaces, halls, and places with triumphal arches for the public
and who print all these books and papers, and who procure and
transport all these pheasants, ortolans, oysters and wines which
are to be eaten and drunk by those who are brought up, educated

and maintained by the working-class, and who, in turn, deceive and prepare for it the worst disasters.

Always the same good-natured, foolish working-folk, who, yawning, showing their white, healthy teeth, childishly and naively pleased at the sight of admirals and presidents in full dress, of flags waving above their heads, and fireworks, and triumphal music : for whom, before they can look round, there will be no more admirals, nor presidents, nor flags, nor music ; but only a damp and empty field of battle, cold, hunger, and pain ; before them a murderous enemy, behind, relentless officers preventing their escape ; blood, wounds, putrefying bodies, and senseless unecessary death.

While, on the other hand, those who have been made much of at Paris and Toulon will be seated, after a good dinner, with glasses of choice wine beside them and cigars between their lips, in a warm cloth tent, marking upon a map with pins such and such places upon which a certain amount of " food for powder " is to be expended—" food " composed of those same foolish people—in order finally to capture this fortified place or the other, and to obtain a certain little ribbon or grade.

VI.

" But nothing of the kind exists ; we have no sanguinary intentions," it is replied. " All that has happened is the expression of mutual sympathy between two nations. What can be amiss in the triumphal and honourable reception of the representatives of a friendly nation by the representatives of another nation ? What can be wrong in this, even if we admit that the alliance is significant of a protection from a dangerous neighbour who threatens Europe with war ?"

It is wrong, because it is false—a most evident and insolent falsehood, inexcusable, iniquitous.

It is false, this suddenly begotten love of Russians for French and French for Russians. And it is false, this insinuation of our dislike to the Germans, and our distrust of them. And more false still is it that the aim of all these indecent and insane orgies is supposed to be the preservation of the peace of Europe.

We are all aware that we neither felt before nor have felt since, any special love for the French, or any animosity towards the Germans.

We are told that Germany has projects against Russia, that the Triple Alliance threatens to destroy our peace and that of Europe and that our alliance with France will secure an equal balance of power and be a guarantee of peace.

In order that such a condition should be attained it would be necessary to make the Powers mathematically equal.

If the preponderance were on the side of the Franco-Russian alliance, the danger would be the same, or even greater, because if Wilhelm, who is at the head of the Triple Alliance, is a menace to peace. France, who cannot be reconciled to the loss of her provinces, would be a still greater menace. The Triple Alliance is called an alliance of peace, whereas for us it proved an alliance of war. Just so now the Franco-Russian alliance can only be viewed truly as an alliance for war.

Moreover, if peace depend upon an even balance of power, how are those units to be defined between which the balance is to be established ?

England asserts that the Franco-Russian alliance is a menace to her security, which necessitates a new alliance on her part. And into precisely how many units is Europe to be divided that this even balance may be attained ?

" Indeed, if there be such a necessity for equilibrium in every society of men, a man stronger than his fellows is already a danger, against which the rest must join defensive alliances.

It is demanded, " What is wrong in France and Russia expressing their mutual sympathies for the preservation of peace ? " The expression is wrong because it is false, and a falsehood once pronounced never ends harmlessly.

The devil " was a murderer from the beginning, and abode not in the truth." Falsehood always lead to murder ; and most of all in such a case as this.

Just what is now taking place occurred before our last Turkish war, when a sudden love on our part was supposed to have been awakened towards certain Slavonic brethren none had heard of for centuries ; though French, Germans, and English always have been, and are, incomparably nearer and dearer to us than a few Bulgarians, Servians, or Montenegrins. And on that occasion just the same enthusiasm, receptions, and solemnities were to be observed, blown into existence by men like Aksakoff and Katkoff, who are already mentioned in Paris as model patriots, Then, as now, the suddenly begotten love of Russ for Slav was only a thing of words.

Then in Moscow as now in Paris when the affair began, people ate, drank, talked nonsense to each other, were much affected by their noble feelings, spoke of union and of peace, passing over in silence the main business—the project against Turkey.

The press goaded on the excitement, and by degress the government took a hand in the game. Servia revolted. Diplomatic notes began to circulate and semi-official articles to appear. The Press lied more and more, invented and gave vent to the irritation ; and in the end Alexander II., who really did yot desire war, was obliged to consent to it and what we know took place, the loss of hundreds of thousands of innocent men, and the brutalising and befooling of millions.

What took place at Paris and Toulon, and has since been fomented by the Press, is evidently leading to a like or a worse calamity.

At first, in the same manner, to the strains of the " Marseillaise " and " God save the Tsar," certain generals and ministers drink to France and Russia in honour of various regiments and fleets ; the Press publishes its falsehoods ; idle crowds of wealthy people, not knowing how to apply their strength and time, chatter patriotic speeches, stirring up animosity against Germany ; and in the end, how peaceful soever Alexander III. may be, circumstances will so unite that he will be unable to avoid war, which will be demanded by all who surround him, by the Press, and, as always seems in such cases, by the entire public opinion of the nation. And before we can look round, the usual ominous absurd proclamation will appear in the papers—

" We, by God's grace, the autocratic great Emperor of All Russia, King of Poland, Grand Duke of Finland, &c., &c., proclaim to all our true subjects, that, for the welfare of these our beloved subjects, bequeathed by God into our care, we have found it our duty before God to send them to slaughter. God be with us."

The bells will peal, long-haired men will dress in golden sacks to pray for successful slaughter. And the old story will begin again, the awful customary acts.

The editors of the daily Press will begin virulently to stir men up to hatred and manslaughter in the name of patriotism, happy in the receipt of an increased income.   Manufacturers, merchants, contractors for military stores will hurry joyously about their business, in the hope of double receipts.

All sorts of Government officials will buzz about, foreseeing a possibility of purloining something more than usual.   The military authorities hurry hither and thither, drawing double pay and rations, and with the expectation of receiving for the slaughter of other men various silly little ornaments which they so highly prize, as ribbons, crosses, orders, and stars.   Idle ladies and gentlemen will make a great fuss, entering their names in advance for the Red Cross Society, and ready to bind up the wounds of those whom their husbands and brothers will mutilate, and they will imagine that in so doing they are performing a most Christian work.

And, smothering despair within their souls by songs, licentiousness, and wine, men will trail along, torn from peaceful labour, from their wives, mothers and children—hundreds of thousands of simple-minded, good-natured men with murderous weapons in their hands—anywhere they may be driven.

They will march, freeze, hunger, suffer sickness, and die from it, or finally come to some place where they will be slain by thousands, or kill thousands themselves with no reason—men whom they have never seen before, and who neither have done nor could do them any mischief.

And when the number of sick, wounded, and killed becomes so great that there are not hands enough left to pick them up, and when the air is so infected with the putrifying scent of the "food for powder" that even the authorities find it disagreeable, a truce will be made, the wounded will be picked up anyhow, the sick will be brought in and huddled together in heaps, the killed will be covered with earth and lime, and once more all the crowd of deluded men will be led on and on till those who have devised the project weary of it, or till those who thought to find it profitable receive their spoil.

And so once more men will be made savage, fierce, and brutal, and love will wane in the world, and the Christianising of mankind, which has already begun, will lapse for scores and hundreds of years.   And so once more the men who reaped profit from it all, will assert with assurance that since there has been a war there must needs have been one, and that other wars must follow, and they will again prepare future generations for a continuance of slaughter, depraving them from their birth.

VII.

Hence, when such patriotic demonstrations as the Toulon festivities take place—though they only constrain from a distance the wills of men, and bind them to those accustomed villainies which are always the outcome of patriotism—everyone who realises the true import of these festivities cannot but protest against what is tacitly included in them. And, therefore, when those gentlemen, the journalists, assert that every Russian sympathises with what took place at Constadt, Toulon, and Paris, and that this alliance for life and death is sealed by the desire of the entire nation ; and when the Russian Minister of Education assures the French Minister that all his brigade of children, clerks, and scientists share his feelings ; or when the commander of a Russian squadron assures the French that all Russia will be grateful to them for their reception, and when arch-priests answer for their flock, and assert that the prayers of Frenchmen for the welfare of the Imperial house are joyously echoed in the hearts of the Russian *Tsar-loving* nation ; and when the Russian Ambassador in Paris, as the representative of the Russian people, states, after a dish of *ortolans à la soubise*, or *logopèdes glacés*, with a glass of grand Moët champagne in his hand, that all Russian hearts, beating in unison with his heart, are filled with sudden and exclusive love for beautiful France—then we, men not yet idiots, regard it as a sacred duty, not only for ourselves, but for tens of millions of Russians, to protest most energetically against such a statement, and to affirm that our hearts do not beat in unison with those of these gentlemen—the journalists, ministers of education, commanders of squadrons, arch-priests, and ambassaders ; but on the contrary, are filled with indignation and disgust at the pernicious falsehood and wrong which, consciously or unconsciously, they are spreading by their words and deeds. Let them drink as much Moët as they please ; let them write articles and make speeches from themselves and for themselves ; but we who regard ourselves as Christians, cannot admit that what all these gentlemen write and say is binding upon us.

This we cannot admit because we know what lies hidden beneath at these tipsy ecstacies, speeches and embracings which resemble, not a confirmation of peace, as we are assured, but rather those orgies and revellings to which criminals are addicted when planning their joint crimes.

VIII.

About four years ago the first swallow of this Toulon spring, a well-known French agitator for a war with Germany, came to Russia to prepare the way for the Franco-Russian alliance, and paid a visit to us in the country. He came to us when we were all engaged cutting the hay crop, and when we had come into lunch and made our guest's acquaintance, he began at once to tell us how he had fought, been taken prisoner, made his escape, and finally pledged himself as a patriot—a fact of which he was evidently proud—never to cease agitating for a war with Germany until the boundaries and g lory of France had been re-established.

All our guest's arguments as to the necessity of an alliance of France with Russia in order to reconstruct the former boundary, power and glory of his country, and to assure our security against the evil intentions of Germany, had no success in our circle.

To his arguments that France could never settle down until she had recaptured her lost provinces, we replied that neither could Russia be at rest till she had been avenged for Jena, and that f the *revanche* of France should happen to be successful, Germany in her turn would desire revenge, and so on without end.

To his arguments that it was the duty of France to recover the sons who had been snatched from her, we replied that the condition of the majority of the working population of Alsace-Lorraine under the rule of Germany had probably suffered no change for the worse since the days when it was ruled by France, and the fact that some of the Alsatians preferred to be registered as Frenchmen and not as Germans, and that he, our guest, wished to re-establish the fame of the French arms, was no reason to renew the awful calamities which a war would cause, or even to sacrifice a single human life.

To his arguments that it was very well for us to talk like that, who had never endured what France had, and that we would speak very differently if the Baltic provinces or Poland were to be taken from us, we replied that the loss of the Baltic provinces or Poland could in no wise be considered as a calamity, but rather as an advantage, as it would decrease the necessity of armed forces and State expenses ; and that from the Christian point of view one can never admit the justice of war, as war demands murder ;

while Christianity not only prohibits all killing, but demands of us the betterment of all men, regarding all men as brothers, without distinction of nationalities.

A Christian nation, we said, which engages in war, ought, in order to be logical, not only to take down the cross from its church steeples, turn the churches to some other use, give the clergy other duties, having first prohibited the preaching of the Gospel, but also ought to abandon all the requirements of morality, which flow from the Christian law.

"*C'est à prendre ou à laisser*," we said. Until Christianity be abolished it is only possible to attract mankind towards war by cunning and fraud, as now practised. We who see this fraud and cunning cannot give way to it.

Since, during this conversation, there was neither music nor champagne, nor anything to confuse our senses, our guest merely shrugged his shoulders, and, with the amiability of a Frenchman, said he was very grateful for the cordial welcome he had experienced in our house, but was sorry that his views were not as well received.

IX.

After this conversation we went out into the hay-field, where our guest, hoping to find the peasants more in sympathy with his ideas, asked me to translate to an old, sickly peasant, Prokophy by name—who, though suffering from severe hernia, was still working energetically, mowing with us—his plan for putting pressure on Germany from both sides, the Russian and the French.

The Frenchman explained this to him graphically, by pressing with his white fingers on either side of the mower's coarse shirt, which was damp with heat.

I well remember Prokophy's good-humoured smile of astonishment when I explained the meaning of the Frenchman's words and action. He evidently took the proposal to squeeze the Germans as a joke, not conceiving that a full-grown and educated man would quietly and soberly speak of war as being desirable.

"Well, but if we squeeze him from both sides," he answered, smiling, giving one pleasantry for another, "he will be fixed too fast to move. We shall have to let him out somewhere."

I translated this answer to my guest.

"Tell him we love the Russians," he said.

These words astonished Prokophy even more than the proposal to squeeze the Germans, and awoke in him a certain feeling of suspicion.

" Whence does he come ? " he inquired.

I replied that he was a wealthy Frenchman.

" And what business has brought him here ? " he asked.

When I replied that the Frenchman had come in the hope of persuading the Russians to enter into an alliance with the French in the event of a war with Germany, Prokophy was clearly entirely displeased, and, turning to the women who were sitting close by on a cock of hay, called out to them, in an angry voice, which unwittingly displayed the feelings which had been aroused in him, to go and stack the rest of the hay.

" Well, you crows," he cried, "you are all asleep! Go and stack ! A nice time for squeezing the Germans ! Look there, the hay has not been turned yet, and it looks as if we might have to begin on the corn on Wednesday." And then, as if afraid of having offended our visitor, he added, smiling good-naturedly and showing his worn teeth, " Better come and work with us, and bring the Germans too. And when we have finished we will have some feasting, and make the Germans join us. They are men like ourselves."

And so saying Prokophy took his hands from the fork of the rake on which he had been leaning, lifted it on to his shoulder, and went off after the women.

" Oh, the dear fellow ! " exclaimed the polite Frenchman, laughing. And thus was concluded for the time his diplomatic mission to the Russian people.

The different aspects of these two men—one shining with freshness and high spirits, dressed in a coat of the latest cut, displaying with his white hands, which had never known labour, how the Germans should be squeezed ; the other coarse, with haydust in his hair, shrunken with hard work, sunburnt, always weary, and, notwithstanding his severe complaint, always at work : Prokophy, with his fingers swollen with toil, in his large home-made trousers, worn-out shoes, and a great heap of hay upon his shoulders, moving slowly along with that careful economy of stride common to all working men—the different aspects of these two men made much clear to me at the time, which has come back to me vividly since the Toulon-Paris festivities.

One of them represented the class fed and maintained by the people's labour, who in return use up that people as "food for powder"; while the other was that very "food for powder" which feeds and maintains those who afterwards so dispose of it.

X.

"But France has lost two provinces—children torn from a beloved mother. And Russia cannot permit Germany to make laws for her and rob her of her historical mission in the East, nor risk the chance of losing, like France, her Baltic provinces, Poland, or the Caucasus.

"And Germany cannot hear of the loss of those advantages which she has won at such a sacrifice. And England will yield to none her naval supremacy."

After such words it is generally supposed that a Frenchman, Russian, German, or Englishman should be ready to sacrifice anything, to regain his lost provinces, establish his influence in the East, secure national unity, or keep his control of the seas.

It is assumed that patriotism is, to start with, a sentiment natural to all men, and that secondly, it is so highly moral a sentiment that it should be induced in all who have it not.

But neither is one nor the other true. I have lived half-a-century amid the Russian people, and in the great mass of labourers, during that period, I have never once seen nor heard any manifestation or expression of this sentiment of patriotism, unless one should count those patriotic phrases which are learned by heart in the army, and repeated from books by the more superficial and degraded of the populace. I have never heard from the people any expression of patriotism, but, on the contrary, I have often listened to expressions of indifference, and even contempt, for any kind of patriotism, by the most venerable and serious of working folk. I have observed the same thing amongst the labouring classes of other nations, and have received confirmation from educated Frenchmen, Germans and Englishmen, from observation of their respective working classes.

The working classes are too much occupied supporting the lives of themselves and of their families, which duty engrosses all their attention, to be able to take an interest in those political questions which are the chief motives of patriotism.

Questions as to the influence of Russia in the East, the unity of

Germany, the recovery by France of her lost provinces, or the concession of such a part of one State to another State, do not interest the working man, not only because, for the most part, he is unacquainted with the circumstances which evoke such questions, but also because the interests of his life are altogether independent of the State and of politics. For a labouring man is altogether indifferent where such-and-such a frontier may be delimitated, to whom Constantinople may belong, whether Saxony or Brunswick shall or shall not be a member of the German Federation, whether Australia or Montebello shall belong to England, or even to what Government they may have to pay taxes, or into what army to send their sons.

But it is always a matter of importance to them to know what taxes they will have to pay, how long to serve in the army, how much to pay for their land, and how much to receive for their labour—all questions entirely independent of State and political interests. This is the reason why, notwithstanding the energetic means employed by Governments to inculcate patriotism, which is not natural to the people, and to destroy Socialism, the latter continues to penetrate further into the labouring masses, whereas patriotism, though so assiduously inculcated, not only makes no headway, but disappears constantly more and more, and is now solely a possession of the upper classes to whom it is profitable. And if, as sometimes happens, that patriotism takes hold of the masses, as lately in Paris, it is only when the masses have been subjected to some special hypnotic influence by the Government and ruling class, and such patriotism only lasts as long as the influence is continued.

Thus, for instance, in Russia, where patriotism, in the form of love for and devotion to the faith, Tsar, and country, is instilled into the people, with extraordinary energy by every means in the hands of the Government—the Church, schools, literature, and every sort of pompous ceremony—the Russian working-man, the hundred millions of the working people, in spite of their undeserved reputation for devotion to faith, Tsar, and country, are a people singularly unduped by patriotism and such devotion.

They are not for the most part, even acquainted with the orthodox official faith to which they are supposed to be so attached, and whenever they do make acquaintance with it they leave it and become rationalists—that is, they adopt a creed which

cannot be attacked and need not he defended; and notwithstanding the constant, energetic insistance of devotion to the Tsar,
they regard in general, all authority founded on violence either
with condemnation or with total indifference; their country, if by
that word anything is meant outside their village and district,
they either do not realise at all, or, if they do, would make no
distinctions between it and other countries. So that where
formerly Russians would emigrate into Austria or Turkey, they
now go with equal indifference to another part of Russia, Turkey,
or China.

XI.

An old friend of mine, who passed the winters alone in the
country while his wife whom he visited from time to time, lived in
Paris, often conversed during the long autumn evenings with his
steward an illiterate but shrewd and venerable peasant, who used
to come to him in the evening to receive his orders, and my friend
once mentioned amongst other things the advantages of the French
system of government compared with our own.   The occasion was
a short time previous to the last Polish insurrection and the inter-
vention of the French Government in our affairs.   At that time
the patriotic Russian Press was burning with indignation at this
interference, and so excited the ruling classes that our political
relations became very strained, and there were rumours of an
approaching war with France.
My friend, having read the papers, explained to this peasant the
misunderstanding between France and Russia; and coming under
the influence of the journal, and being an old military man, said
that were war to be declared he would re-enter the army and fight
with France.   At that time a *revanche* against the French for
Sebastapol was considered a necessity by patriotic Russians.
"For what should we fight with them?" asked the peasant.
"Why how can we permit France to dictate to us?"
"Well, you said yourself that they were better governed than
we," replied the peasant quite seriously; let them arrange things
as well in Russia."
And my friend told me that he was so taken aback by this
argument that he did not know what to reply and burst into
laughter, as one who has just awaked from a delusive dream.
The same argument may be heard from every Russian workman

if he has not come under the hypnotic influence of the Government.   People speak of the Russian's love for his faith, Tsar, and
countr y ; and yet a single community of peasants could not be
found in Russia which would hesitate one moment had they to
choose of two places for emigration—one in Russia, under the
" Father-Tsar " (as he is termed only in books), and the holy
orthodox faith of his idolized country, but with less or worse land ;
and the other without the " White-father-Tsar," and without the
orthodox faith, somewhere outside Russia in Prussia, China,
Turkey, Austria, only with more and better land—the choice would
be in favour of the latter as we have often had opportunity to
observe.

The question as to who shall govern him (and he knows that
under any Government he will be equally robbed) is for the Russian
peasant of infinitely less significance than the question (setting
aside even the matter of water), is the clay soft and will cabbage
thrive in it ?

But it might be supposed that this indifference on the part of
Russians arises from the fact that any Government under which
they might live would be an improvement on their own, because
in Europe there is none worse.   But that is not so ; for as far as I
can judge, one may witness the same indifference among English,
Dutch and German peasants emigrating to America, and among
the various nationalities which have emigrated to Russia.

Passing from the control of one European Government to
another—from Turkish to Austrian, or from French to German—
alters so slightly the position of the genuine working classes that
in no case would the change excite any discontent, if only
ct be not effected artificially by the Government and the ruling
ilasses.

XII.

Usually, for a proof of the existence of patriotism one is referred
to the display of patriotic sentiment by the people on certain
solemn occasions, as in Russia, at the coronation of the Tsar, or
his reception after the railway accident on October 17 ; in France,
on the proclamation of war with Prussia ; in Germany at the
rejoicings after the war ; or during the Franco-Russian festivities.

But one ought to take into consideration the way these manifestations are arranged.   In Russia, for example, during every pro-

gress of the Emperor, delegates are commanded to appear from every peasant community, and materials requisitioned for the reception and welcome of the Tsar.

The enthusiasm of the crowd is for the most part artificially prepared by those who require it, and the degree of enthusiasm exhibited by the crowd is only a clue to the refinements in the art of those who organise such exhibitions. The art has been practised for long, hence the specialists in it have acquired great adroitness in its preparation.

When Alexander II. was still heir apparent, and commanded, as is usual, the Préobajensky Regiment, he once paid an after-dinner visit to the regiment, which was in camp at the time.

As soon as his calèche came in sight, the soldiers, who were only in their shirts at the time, ran out to welcome their "august commander," as the phrase is, with such enthusiasm, that they all followed the carriage, and many, while running, made the sign of the cross, gazing upon the prince. All who witnessed this reception were deeply moved by this simple attachment of the Russian soldier to the Tsar and his son, and by the genuinely religious, and evidently spontaneous, enthusiasm expressed in their faces, movements, and especially by the signing of the cross.

And yet all this had been artificially prepared in the following manner :—

After a review on the previous day the Prince told the commander of the brigade that he would revisit the regiment on the following day.

"When are we to expect your Imperial Highness?"

"Probably in the evening, only, pray, do not expect me: and let there be no preparation."

As soon as the Prince was gone, the commander of the brigade called all the captains of companies together, and gave orders that on the following day all the men should have clean shirts, and the moment the Prince's carriage should come in sight (special signalmen were to be sent out to give warning of it) everyone should run to meet it, and with shouts of "Hurrah!" run after it, and, moreover, that every tenth man in each company should cross himself whilst running. The colour-sergeants drew up the companies, and told off every tenth man to cross himself. "One, two, three, ... eight, nine, ten. Sidorenko, you are to cross yourself. One, two, three . . . . Ivanoff, to cross yourself."

Thus, what was ordered was accomplished, and an impression of spontaneous enthusiasm was produced upon the Prince and upon all who saw it, even upon the soldiers and officers, and even upon the commander of the brigade himself.

The same thing is done, though less peremptorily, wherever patriotic manifestations take place. Thus the Franco-Russian festivities, which strike us as the spontaneous outcome of the nation's feelings, did not happen of their own accord, but were very cleverly prepared and arranged for by the foresight of the French Government.

As soon as the advent of the Russian fleet was settled, "at once," I again quote from that official organ, the *Village Review*, "not only in large towns upon the somewhat lengthy route from Toulon to Paris, but in many places far removed from it, the organisation of festivities was commenced by special committees.

"Contributions were everywhere received to defray the expenses of the welcome. Many towns sent deputations to our Ambassador in Paris, praying that our sailors should be permitted to visit them even for a day or an hour.

"The municipalities of all those towns which our sailors were directed to visit voted vast sums of money—more than a hundred thousand roubles —to promote various festivities and merrymakings, and expressed their readiness to devote even a larger sum to the purpose, if necessary, to make the welcome as magnificent as possible.

"In Paris itself, in addition to the sum voted by the town municipality, a large amount was collected in voluntary contributions by a private committee for the series of entertainments, and the French Government decreed over a hundred thousand roubles for the reception of the Russian visitors by the Ministers and other authorities. In many places which our sailors were unable to visit it was decided to keep October 1 as a festal day in honour of Russia. A number of towns and departments decided to send to Toulon and Paris special deputies to welcome the Russian visitors, to give them presents in memory of France, or to send them addresses and telegrams of welcome.

"It was decided everywhere to regard October 1 as a national feast day, and to give a day's holiday to all the school-children, and in Paris two days.

"Soldiers undergoing certain sentences were pardoned, in order that they might remember with thankfulness the joyous October 1 in the annals of France.

" To enable the public who wished to visit Toulon to participate in the reception of the Russian squadron, the railways reduced their fares to one-half, and arranged for special trains."

And thus when, by a series of measures undertaken everywhere and at the same time—always thanks to the power in its hands at the command of the Government—a certain portion of the people, chiefly the froth, the town crowds, is brought into an unnaturally excited state, it is said. Look at this spontaneous action of the will of the whole nation.

Such manifestations as those of Toulon and Paris, as those which take place in Germany at the receptions of the Emperor or of Bismarck, or at the manœuvres in Lothringen, as those which are always repeated in Russia at all pompously arranged receptions, only prove that the means of exciting a nation artificially which are at present in the hands of the Governments and ruling classes, can always evoke any patriotic manifestations they choose, and afterwards label it as the outcome of the patriotic sentiments of the people.

Nothing, on the contrary, proves so clearly the absence of patriotism in the people, as these same excessive measures now used for its artificial excitement and the small results attained with so much effort.

If patriotic sentiments are so natural to a people, why then is it not allowed to express itself of its own accord, instead of being stirred up by every ordinary and extraordinary means ?

If only the attempt were made for a time in Russia to abolish at the coronation of the Tsar the taking of the oath of allegiance by the people, the solemn repetition of the prayers for the Tsar during every church service ; to forego the festivals of his birth and saints' days, with illuminations, the pealing of bells and compulsory idleness, to cease the public exhibition of his portrait, and in prayer-books, calendars, and books of study, to print no more the family names of himself and of his family, and of even the pronouns alluding to them, in large letters ; to cease to honour him by special books and papers published for that purpose ; to put an end to imprisonment for the least word of disrespect concerning him—let us see these things altered for a time, and then we could know how far it is inherent in the people, in the genuine,

c

working-class. Prokophy and Ivan the steward, as they are always assured, and as every foreigner is assured, idolise the Tsar, who one way or another betrays them into the hands of landowners and of the rich in general.

So it is in Russia. But if only in like manner the ruling classes in Germany, France, Italy, England, and America were to do what they so persistently accomplish in the inculcation of patriotism, attachment and obedience to the existing Government, we should be able to see how far this supposed patriotism is natural to the nations of our time.

From infancy, by every possible means—class-books, church services, sermons, speeches, books, papers, songs, poetry, monuments—the people is stupefied in one direction; and then either by force or by bribe, several thousands of the people are assembled, and when these, joined by the idlers always present at every sight, to the sound of cannon and music, and inflamed by the glitter and brilliance about them, will commence to shout out what others are shouting in front of them, we are told that this is the expression of the sentiment of the entire nation.

But, in the first place, these thousands, or even tens of thousands, who shout something or other on these occasions are only a mere ten-thousandth part of the whole nation; and, in the second, of these ten thousand men who shout and wave their hats, the greater, part, if not collected by the authorities, as in Russia, is artificially attracted by some kind of bait; and in the third place, of all these thousands there are scarcely a hundred who know the real meaning of what is taking place, and the majority would shout and wave their hats in just the same way for an exactly opposite intention; and in the fourth place, the police is present with power to quiet and silence at once any who might attempt to shout in a fashion not desired nor demanded by Government, as was energetically done during the Franco-Russian festivities.

In France, war with Russia welcomed with just the same zest in the reign of Napoleon I., then the war against Alexander I., then that of the allied forces under Napoleon III.; the Bourbons have been welcomed in the same fashion as the House of Orleans, the Republic, Napoleon III., and Boulanger. And in Russia the same welcome has been accorded to Peter, Catherine, Paul, Alexander, Constantine, Nicolas, the Duke of Leichtenberg, the "brotherly Slavonians," the King of Prussia, the French sailors, and any others the authorities desired to welcome. And just the same thing has taken place in England, America, Germany, and Italy.

What is called patriotism in our time is, on the one hand, only a certain disposition of mind, constantly produced and sustained in the minds of the people in a direction desired by the existing Government by schools, religion, and a subsidised Press ; and on the other hand it is a temporary excitement of the lowest stratum, morally and intellectually, of the people, produced by special means by the ruling classes, and finally acclaimed as the permanent expression of the people's will.

The patriotism of States oppressed by a foreign Power presents no exception. It is equally unnatural to the working masses, and artificially induced by the higher classes.

XIII.

" But if the common people have no sentiment of patriotism it is because they have not yet developed this elevated feeling natural to every educated man. If they do not possess this nobility of sentiment, it must be cultivated in them. And it is this the Government does."

So say, generally, the ruling classes, with such assurance that patriotism is a noble feeling, and that the simple populace who are ignorant of it, think themselves, in consequence at fault, and try to persuade themselves that they really possess it, or at least pretend to have it.

But what is this elevated sentiment which, according to the opinon of the ruling classes, must be educated in the people ?

The sentiment, in its simplest definition, is merely the preference for one's own country or nation above the country or nation of any one else ; a sentiment perfectly expressed in the German patriotic song, " Deutschland, Deutschland über Alles," in which one need only substitute for the first two words, " Russland," " Frankreich," " Italien," or the name of any other country, to obtain a formula of the elevated sentiment of patriotism for that country.

It is quite possible that this sentiment is both of use to, and to be desired by the Government, and of service to the unity of the State, but one must see that this sentiment is by no means an elevated one, but on the contrary, very stupid and immoral. Stupid, because if every country were to consider itself superior to others, it is evident that all but one would be in error, and immoral because it leads all who possess it to aim at benefiting their own country or nation at the expense of every other—an inclination exactly at variance with the fundamental moral law, which all admit " Do not unto others as you would not wish them to do unto you."

Patriotism may have been a virtue in the ancient world when it compelled men to serve the highest idea of those days,—the fatherland. But how can patriotism be a virtue in these days when it requires of men an ideal exactly opposite to that of our religion and morality—an admission not of the equality and fraternity of all men but of the dominance of one country or nations over all others? But not only is this sentiment no virtue in our times, but it is indubitably a vice ; for this sentiment of patriotism cannot now exist, because there is neither material nor moral foundation for its conception.

Patriotism might have had some meaning in the ancient world, more or less uniform in composition, professing one national faith and subject to the unrestrained authority of its great and adored sovereign representing as it were, an island in an ocean of barbarians who sought to overflow it.

It is conceivable that in such circumstances patriotism—the desire of protection from barbarian assault, ready not only to destroy the social order, but threatening it with plunder, slaughter, captivity, slavery, and the violation of its women—was a natural feeling : and it is conceivable that men, in order to defend themselves and their fellow-countrymen, might prefer their own nation to any other, and cherish a feeling of hatred towards the surrounding barbarians, and destroy them for self-protection.

But what significance can this feeling have in these Christian days ?

On what grounds and for what reason can a man of our time follow this example—a Russian, for instance, kill Frenchmen ; or a Frenchman, Germans—when he is well aware, however un-educated he may be, that the men of the country or nation against whom his patriotic animosity is excited are no barbarians, but men, Christians, like himself, often of the same faith as himself, and, like him, desirous of peace and the peaceful interchange of abour ; and besides, bound to him, for the most part, either by the interest of a common effort, or by mercantile or spiritual endeavours, or even by both ? So that very often people of one country are nearer and more needful to their neighbours than are these latter to one another, as in the case of labourers in the service of foreign employers of labour, of commercial houses, scientists and the followers of art.

Moreover, the very conditions of life are now so changed, that what we call fatherland, and which we are asked to distinguish from everything else, has ceased to be clearly defined, as with the ancients, when men of the same country were of one nationality one state, and one religion.

The patriotism of an Egyptian, a Jew, a Greek is comprehensible who in defending his country defended his religion, his nationality, his fatherland, and his state.

But in what terms can one express to-day the patriotism of an Irishman in the United States, who by his religion belongs to Rome, by his nationality, to Ireland, by his citizenship to the United States? In the same position is a Bohemian in Austria, a Pole in Russia, Prussia, or Austria ; a Hindoo, in England; a Tartar or Armenian in Russia or Turkey. Not to mention the people of these particular conquered nations, the people of the most homogeneous countries, Russia, France, Prussia, can no longer possess the sentiment of patriotism which was natural to the ancients, because very often the chief interests of their lives— of the family, for instance, where a man is married to a woman of another nationality—commercial, where his capital is invested abroad ; spiritual, scientific or artistic—are no longer contained within the limits of his country, but outside it, in the very State, perhaps, against which his patriotic animosity is being excited.

But patriotism is chiefly impossible to-day, because, however much we may have endeavoured during 1800 years to conceal the meaning of Christianity, it has nevertheless leaked into our lives, and controls them to such an extent that the dullest and most unrefined of men must see to-day the complete nonconformity of patriotism with the moral law by which we live.

XIV.

Patriotism was a necessity in the formation and consolidation of powerful States composed of different nationalities and acting in mutual defence against barbarians. But as soon as Christian enlightenment transformed these States from within, giving to all an equal standing, patriotism became not only needless, but the sole impediment to a union between nations for which, by reason of their Christian consciousness, they were prepared.

Patriotism to-day is the cruel tradition of an outlived period, which exists not merely by its inertia, but because the Governments and ruling classes, aware that not their power only, but their very existence, depends upon it, excite and maintain it among the people persistently, both by cunning and violence.

Patriotism to-day is like a scaffolding which was needful once to raise the walls of the building, but which, though it presents the only obstacle to the house being inhabited, is none the less retained, because its existence is of profit to certain persons.

For a long while there has not been and cannot be any reason for dissension between Christian nations. It is even impossible to imagine, how and for what, Russian and German workmen, peacefully and conjointly working on the frontiers or in the capitals, should quarrel. And much less easily can one imagine animosity between some Kazan peasant who supplies Germans with wheat, and a German who supplies him with scythes and machines.

It is the same between French, German, and Italian workmen. And it would be even ridiculous to speak of the possibility of a quarrel between men of science, art and letters of different nationalities, who have the same objects of common interest independent of nationalities or of Governments.

But the various Governments cannot leave the nations in peace, because the chief, if not the sole justification for the existence of Governments is the pacification of nations, and the settlement of their hostile relationships. Hence Governments evoke such hostile relationships under the aspect of patriotism, in order to exhibit their powers of pacification. Somewhat like a gipsy, who having put some pepper under a horse's tail and beaten it in its stall, brings it out, and hanging on to the reins pretends that he can hardly control the excited animal.

We are told that Governments are very careful to maintain peace between nations. How then do they maintain it? People live on the Rhine in peaceful communication with each other. Suddenly, owing to certain quarrels and intrigues between kings and emperors a war commences; and we learn that the French Government has considered it necessary to regard this peaceful people as Frenchmen. Centuries pass, the population has become accustomed to their position when animosity again begins amongst the Governments of the great nations, and a war is started upon the most empty pretext, because the German Government considers it necessary to regard this population as Germans: and between all Frenchmen and Germans is kindled a mutual feeling of ill-will.

Or else Germans and Russians live in friendly fashion on their frontiers, pacifically exchanging the results of their labour; when a of sudden those same institutions, which only exist to maintain the peace of nations, begin to quarrel, are guilty of, one stupidity after another, and finally are unable to invent anything better than a most childish method of self-punishment in order to have their own way, and do a bad turn to their opponent, which in this case is especially easy, as those who arrange a war of tariffs are not the sufferers from it ; it is others who suffer and so arrange such a war of tariffs as took place not long ago between Russia and Germany. And so between Russians and Germans a feeling of animosity is fostered, which is still more inflamed by the Franco Russian festivities, and may lead at one moment or another to a bloody war.

I have mentioned these last two examples of the influence of a Government over the people used to excite their animosity against another people, because they have occurred in our times : but in all history there is no war which was not hatched by a Government independent of the interests of the people, to whom war is always pernicious even when successful.

The Government assures the people that they are in danger from the invasion of another nation, or from foes in their midst, and that the only way to escape this danger is by slavish obedience of the people to their Government. This fact is seen most prominently during revolutions and dictatorships, but it exists always and everywhere that the power of the Government exists. Every Government explains its existence, and justifies its deeds of violence by the argument that if it did not exist the condition of things would be very much worse. After assuring the people of its danger the Government subordinates it to control, and when in this condition compels it to attack other nations. And thus the assurance of the Government is corroborated in the eyes of the people, as to the danger of attack from other nations, " Divide et impera."

Patriotism in its simplest, clearest and most indubitable signification is nothing else but a means of obtaining for the rulers their ambitions and covetous desires, and for the ruled the abdication of human dignity, reason and conscience, and a slavish enthralment to those in power. And as such it is recommended wherever it may be preached.

Patriotism is slavery.

Those who preach peace by arbitration argue thus. Two animals cannot divide their prey otherwise than by fighting ; as also is the case with children, savages and savage nations. But reasonable people settle their differences by argument, persuasion, and by referring the decision of the question to other impartial and reasonable persons. So the nations should act to-day. This argument seems quite correct. The nations of our time have reached the period of reasonableness, have no animosity towards each other, and might decide their differences in a peaceful fashion.

But this argument applies only so far as it has reference to the people and only to the people who are not under the control of a Government. But the people that subordinate themselves to a Government cannot be reasonable, because this subordination is in itself a sign of a want of reason.

How can we speak of the reasonableness of men who promise in advance to accomplish everything, including murder, that the Government—that is, certain men who have attained a certain position—may command ? Men who can accept such obligations, and resignedly subordinate themselves to anything that may be prescribed by persons unknown to them in St. Petersburg, Vienna, Berlin, Paris, cannot be considered reasonable ; and the Governments, that is those who are in possession of such power, can still less be considered reasonable, and cannot but misuse it, and become dazed by such insane and dreadful power.

This is why peace between nations cannot be attained by reasonable means, by conventions, arbitration, and so forth, as long as the subordination of the people to the Goverment continues, a condition always unreasonable and always pernicious.

But the subordination of people to Governments will exist as long as patriotism exists, because all governmental authority is founded upon patriotism, that is upon the readiness of people to subordinate themselves to authority in order to defend their nation, country, or state from dangers which are supposed to threaten.

The power of the French kings over their people before the

Revolution was founded upon patriotism; upon it too was based the power of the Consistory of Public Welfare after the Revolution; upon it the power of Napoleon, was erected, both as Consul and as Emperor; upon it, after the downfall of Napoleon, was based the power of the Bourbons, then that of the Republic, Louis Philippe, and again of the Republic; then of Napoleon III., and again of the Republic, and upon it finally rested the power of M. Boulanger.

It is dreadful to say so, but there is not, nor has there been, any conjoint violence of some people against others which was not accomplished in the name of patriotism. In its name the Russians fought the French, and the French the Russians, Russians and French are preparing to fight the Germans, and the Germans to wage war on both sides.

And such is the case not only with wars. In the name of patriotism the Russians stifle the Poles, the Germans persecute the Slavonians, the men of the Commune killed those of Versailles, and those of Versailles the men of the Commune.

XV.

It would seem that, owing to the spread of education, of speedier locomotion, of greater intercourse between different nations, to the widening of literature, and chiefly to the decrease of danger from other nations, the fraud of patriotism ought daily to become more difficult and at length impossible to practice.

But the truth is that this same spread of general external education, facilitated locomotion, intercourse, and widening of literature, being captured by, and constantly more and more under the control of Government, confers on the latter such possibilities of exciting a feeling of mutual animosity between nations, that in degree as the uselessness and harmfulness of patriotism has become manifest, so also has increased the power of the Government and ruling class to excite patriotism among the people.

The difference between that which was and that which is consists solely in the fact that now a much larger number of men participate in the advantages which patriotism confers on the upper classes, hence a much larger number of men are employed in spreading and sustaining this astounding superstition.

The more difficult the Government finds it to retain its power, the more numerous are the men who share it.

In former times a small band of rulers held the reins of power, emperors, kings, dukes, their soldiers and assistants; whereas now the power and its profits are shared not alone by Government officials and by the clergy, but by capitalists—great and small, landowners, bankers, members of Parliament, professors, village officials, men of science, and even artists, but particularly by authors and journalists.

And all these people, consciously, or unconsciously, spread the deceit of patriotism, which is indispensable to them if the profits of their position are to be preserved.

And the fraud, thanks to the means for its propagation, and to the participation in it of a much larger number of people, having become more powerful, is continued so successfully, that, notwithstanding the increased difficulty of deceiving, the extent to which the people are deceived is the same as ever.

A hundred years ago the uneducated classes, who had no idea of what their Government was composed, or by what nations they were surrounded, blindly obeyed those local Government officials and nobles by whom they were enslaved, and it was sufficient for the Government, by bribes and rewards, to remain on good terms with these nobles and officials, in order to squeeze from the people all that was required.

Whereas now, when the people can, for the most part, read, know more or less of what their Government is composed, and what nations surround them; when working men constantly and easily move from place to place, bringing back information of what is happening in the world, the simple demand that the orders of the Government must be accomplished is not sufficient; it is needful as well to cloud those true ideas about life which the people have, and to inculcate unnatural ideas as to the condition of their existence, and the relationship to it of other nations.

And so, thanks to the development of literature, reading and the facilities of travel, Governments which have their agents everywhere, by means of statutes, sermons, schools, and the Press, inculcate everywhere upon the people the most savage and erroneous ideas as to their utility, the relationship of nations, their quatities and intentions; and the people, so crushed by labour that they have neither the time nor the power to deliberate upon and test the truth of the ideas which are forced upon them or of demands made upon them in the name of their welfare, put themselves unmurmuringly under the yoke.

Whereas working men who have freed themselves from unremitting labour and become educated, and who have therefore, it might be supposed, the power of seeing through the fraud which is practised upon them are subjected to such a coercion of threats, bribes, and all the hypnotic influence of Governments, that, almost without exception, they desert to the side of the Government, and by entering some well paid and profitable employment as priest, schoolmaster, or other official, become participators in spreading the deceit which is destroying their comrades.

It is as though nets were laid at the entrances to education, in which those who, by some means or other, escape from the masses bowed down by labour are inevitably caught.

At first, when one understands the cruelty of all this deceit, one feels indignant in spite of oneself against those who from personal ambition or greedy advantage propagate this cruel fraud which destroys the souls as well as the bodies of men, and one feels inclined to accuse them of a sly craftiness; but the fact is that they are deceitful with no wish to deceive, but because they cannot be otherwise. And they deceive, not as Machiavelli, but with no consciousness of their deceit, and usually with the naïve assurance that they are doing something excellent and elevated, a view in which they are persistently encouraged by the sympathy and approval of all who surround them.

It is true that, being dimly aware that on this fraud is founded their power and advantageous position, they are unconsciously drawn toward it; but their action is not based on any desire to delude the people, but because they believe it to be of service to the people.

Thus emperors, kings, and their ministers, with all their coronations, manœuvres, reviews, visiting each other, dressing up in various uniforms, going from place to place, and deliberating with serious faces as to how they may keep peace between nations supposed to be inimical to each other—nations who would never dream of quarreling—feel quite sure that what they are doing is very reasonable and useful.

In the same way the various ministers, diplomatists, and officials—dressed up in uniforms, with all sorts of ribbons and crosses, writing and docketing with great care, upon the best paper, their hazy, involved, altogether needless communications, advice, projects—are quite assured that, without their activity, the entire existence of nations would halt or become deranged.

In the same manner military men, got up in ridiculous costumes, arguing seriously with what rifle or cannon men can be most expeditiously destroyed, are quite certain that their field days and reviews are most important and essential to the people.

So likewise the priests, journalists, writers of patriotic songs and class books, who preach patriotism and receive liberal remuneration, are equally satisfied.

And no doubt the organisers of festivities—like the Franco-Russian fêtes—are sincerely affected while pronouncing their patriotic speeches and toasts.

All these people do what they are doing unconsciously, because they must ; all their life being founded upon deceit, and because they know not how to do anything else : and coincidently these same acts call forth the sympathy and approbation of all those people amongst whom they are done. More than this, being all linked together, they approve and justify each other's acts—emperor and king those of the soldiers, officials and clergy ; and these latter in their turn the acts of emperor and king. The populace, and especially the town populace, seeing nothing comprehensible in what is being done by all these men, unwittingly ascribe to them a special, almost a supernatural, significance.

The people see, for instance, that a triumphal arch is being erected ; that men bedeck themselves with crowns, uniforms, robes ; that fireworks are let off, cannons fired, bells rung, regiments paraded with their bands ; that papers, telegrams, messengers fly from place to place ; and being unable to believe that all this is being done (as is indeed the case) without the slightest necessity, attribute to it all a special mysterious significance, and gaze with shouts and hilarity or with silent awe. And reciprocally, this hilarity or silent awe confirms the assurance of those people who are responsible for all these foolish deeds. .

So, for instance, not long ago, Wilhelm II. ordered a new throne for himself, with some special kind of ornamentation, and having dressed up in a white uniform, with a cuirass, tight breeches, and a helmet with a bird on the top, and enveloped himself in a red mantle, came out to his subjects, and sat down on this new throne, perfectly assured that his act was most necessary and important; and his subjects not only saw nothing ridiculous in it, but thought the sight most imposing.

XVI.

For some time the power of the Government over the people has not been maintained by force, as was the case when one nation conquered another and ruled it by force of arms, or when the rulers of an unarmed people had separate legions of janissaries or guards.

The power of the Government has for some time been maintained by what is termed public opinion.

A public opinion exists that patriotism is a fine moral sentiment, and that it is right and our duty to regard one's own nation, one's own State as the best in the world; and flowing naturally from this public opinion is another, namely, that it is right and our duty to acquiesce in the control of a Government over ourselves, to subordinate ourselves to it, to serve in the army and submit ourselves to discipline, to give our earnings to the Government in the form of taxes, to submit to the decisions of the law-courts, and to consider the edicts of the Government as divinely right. And when such public opinion exists, a strong govermental power is formed possessing milliards of money, an organised mechanism of administration, the postal service, telegraph, telephone, army, law-courts, police, submissive clergy schools, even the Press; and this power maintains in the people the public opinion which it finds necessary to its own existence.

The power of the Government is maintained by public opinion, and with this power the Government, by means of its organs—its officials, law-courts, schools, churches, even the Press—can always maintain the public opinion which they need. Public opinion constitutes the power, and the power public opinion. And there appears to be no escape from this position.

Nor indeed would there be, if public opinion were something fixed, unchangeable, and Governments able to manufacture the exact opinion they were in need of.

But, fortunately, such is not the case; and public opinion is not, to begin with, permanent, unchangeable, stationary; but, on the contrary, constantly changing, moving with the advance of humanity; and public opinion not only cannot be produced at will by a Government, but is that which produces Governments and gives them power, or deprives them of it.

It may seem that public opinion is at present stationary, and the same to-day as it was ten years ago ; that in relation to certain questions it merely fluctuates, but returns again—as when it replaces a monarchy with a republic, and then the republic with a monarchy; but it has only that appearance when we examine merely the external manifestation of public opinion which is produced artificially by the Government.

But we need only take public opinion in its relation to the life of mankind to see that, as with the day or the year, it is never stagnant, but always proceeds along the way by which all humanity advances, as, notwithstanding delays and hesitations, the spring advances by the same path as the sun.

So that, although, judging from external appearances, the position of European nations to-day is almost as it was fifty years ago, the relationship of the nations to these appearances is quite different from what it was then.

Though the same rulers, troops, taxes, luxury and poverty, Catholicism, orthodoxy, Lutheranism, exist now as then ; in former times these existed because demanded by public opinion, *whereas* now they exist only because the Governments artificially *maintain* what was once a vital public opinion.

If we as seldom remark this movement of public opinion as we notice the movement of water in a river when descending ourselves with the current, this is because the imperceptible changes in public opinion influence ourselves as well.

Constant and persistent movement is in the nature of public opinion. If it appears to us to be stationary it is because there are always some who have utilised a certain phase of public opinion for their own profit, and who, in consequence, use every effort to give it an appearance of permanence, and to conceal the manifestations of real opinion, which is already alive, though not yet perfectly expressed, in the consciousness of men. And such people, who adhere to the outworn opinion and conceal the new one, are at the present time those who compose Governments and ruling classes, and who preach patriotism as an indispensable condition of human life.

The means which these people can control are immense ; but as public opinion is constantly pouring in upon them their efforts must in the end be in vain: the old falls into decrepitude, the new grows.

The longer the manifestations of nascent public opinion is restrained, the more it accumulates, the more energetically will i burst forth.

Governments and ruling classes try with all their strength to conserve that old public opinion of patriotism upon which their power rests, and to smother the expression of the new, which would destroy it.

But to preserve the old and to check the new is possible only up to a certain point ; just as, only to a certain extent, is it possible to check running water with a dam.

However much Governments may try to arouse in the people a public opinion, of the past unnatural to them, as to the merit and virtue of patriotism, those of our day believe in patriotism no longer, but espouse more and more the solidarity and brotherhood of nations.

Patriotism does not promise any future that is not terrible, but the brotherhood of nations represents an ideal which is becoming ever more intelligible and more desirable to humanity. Hence the progress of mankind from the old outworn opinion to the new must inevitably take place. This progression is as inevitable as the falling in the spring of the last dry leaves and the appearance of the new from swollen buds.

And the longer this transition is delayed, the more inevitable it becomes, and the more evident its necessity.

And indeed, one has only to remember what we profess, both as Christians and merely as men of our day, those fundamental moralities by which we are directed in our social, family, and personal existence, and the position in which we place ourselves in the name of patriotism, in order to see what a degree of contradiction we have placed between our conscience and what, thanks to an energetic Government influence in this direction, we regard as our public opinion.

One has only thoughtfully to examine the most ordinary demands of patriotism, which are expected of us as the most simple and natural affair, in order to understand to what extent these requirements are at variance with that real public opinion which we already share. We all regard ourselves as free, educated humane men, or even as Christians, and yet we are all in such a

position that were Wilhelm to-morrow to become offended by
Alexander, or Mr. N. or M. to write a lively article on the Eastern
Question, or Prince So-and-So to plunder some Bulgarians or
Servians, or some Queen or Empress to be put out by something or
other, all we educated humane Christians must go and kill people
of whom we have no knowledge, and towards whom we are as
amicably disposed as to the rest of the world.

And if such an event has not come to pass, it is owing, we are
assured, to the love of peace which controls Alexander, or because
Nicolas Alexandrovitch has married the grand-daughter of
Victoria.

But if another happened to be in the room of Alexander, or if
the disposition of Alexander himself were to alter, or if Nicolas
Alexandrovitch had married Amalia instead of Alice, we
should rush at each other like wild beasts, and rip up each other's
bellies.

Such is the supposed public opinion of our time, and such arguments are coolly repeated in every Liberal and advanced organ
of the Press.

If we, Christians for a thousand years, have not already cut each
other's throats, it is merely because Alexander III. does not
permit us to.

But this is awful!

XVII.

No feats of heroism are needed to achieve the greatest and most
important changes in the existence of humanity; neither the
armament of millions of soldiers nor the construction of new roads
and machines, nor the arrangement of exhibitions, nor the organisation of workmen's unions, nor revolutions, nor barricades, nor
explosions, not the perfection of aërial navigation; but a change
in public opinion.

And to accomplish this change no exertions of the mind are
needed, nor the refutation of anything in existence, nor the inven-
tion of any extraordinary novelty; it is only needful that we should
not succumb to the erroneous, already defunct, public opinion of
the past, which Governments have induced artificially; it is only
needful that each individual should say what he really feels or
thinks, or at least, that he should not say what he does not think.

And if only a small body of the people were to do so at once, of their own accord, outworn public opinion would fall off us of itself, and a new living real opinion would assert itself. And when public opinion should thus have changed without the slightest effort, the internal condition of men's lives which so torments them would change likewise of its own accord.

One is ashamed to say how little is needed for all men to be delivered from those calamities which now oppress them : it is only needful not to lie.

Let people only be superior to the falsehood which is instilled into them ; let them decline to say what they neither feel nor think, and at once such a revolution of all the organisation of our life will take place as could not be attained by all the efforts of revolutionists during centuries even were complete power within their hands.

Could people only believe that strength is not in force but in truth, could they only not shrink from it either in word or deed, not say what they do not think, not do what they regard as foolish and as wrong !

" But what is of so grave importance in shouting Long live France ! or, Hurrah for some emperor, king, or conqueror ? " Or, " Why is the writing of an article in defence of the Franco-Russian alliance, or of the war of tariffs, or in condemnation of Germans, Russians, or Englishmen, of such moment ? " Or, " What is of such moment in attendance at some patriotic festivity, or in drinking the health and making a speech in favour of people whom one does not love, and with whom one has no business ?" Or, " What is of such importance in admitting the use and excellence of treaties and alliances, or in keeping silence when one's own nation is belauded in one's hearing, and other nations abused and maligned; or when Catholicism, Orthodoxy, and Lutheranism are bepraised ; or some hero of war as Napoleon, Peter, Boulanger, or Skobeleff, is admired ? "

All these things seem so unimportant. Yet in these ways which seem unimportant to us, in our refraining from them, in our proving, as far as we can, the unreasonableness that is apparent to us, in this is our chief, our irresistible might, of which that unconquerable force is composed which constitutes real genuine public opinion, that opinion which, while itself advancing, moves all humanity.

The Governments know this, and tremble before this force, and strive in every way they can to counteract or become possessed of it.

D

They know that strength is not in force, but in the action of the mind, and in its clear expression, and, therefore, they are more afraid of the expression of independent thought than of armies ; hence they institute cenorships, bribe the Press, and monopolise the control of religion and of the schools.   But the spiritual force which moves the world eludes them ; it is neither in books nor in papers ; it cannot be trapped, and is always free ; it is in the depths of consciousness of mankind.   The most powerful force of freedom which cannot be imprisoned is that which asserts itself in the soul of man when he is alone, and in the sole presence of himself reflects on the facts of the universe, and then naturally communicates his thoughts to wife, brother, friend, with all those with whom he comes in contract, and from whom he would regard it as sinful to conceal the truth.

No milliards of roubles, no millions of troops, no organization, wars, nor revolutions will produce what the simple expression of a free man may, on what he regards as just, independently of what exists or was instilled into him.

One free man will say with truth what he thinks and feels amongst thousands of men who by their acts and words attest exactly the opposite.   It would seem that he who sincerely expressed his thought must remain alone, whereas it generally happens that everyone else, or the majority at least have been thinking and feeling the same things but without expressing them.

And that which yesterday was the novel opinion of one man, to-day becomes the general opinion of the majority.

And as soon as this opinion is established, immediately by imperceptible degrees, but beyond power of frustration, the conduct of mankind begins to alter.

Whereas, at present, every man, even if free, asks himself " What can I do alone against all this ocean of evil and deceit which overwhelms us ? Why should I express my opinion ? Why indeed possess one? It is better not to reflect on these misty and involved questions.   Perhaps these contradictions are an inevitable condition of our existence.   And why should I struggle alone with all the evil in the world ?   Is it not better to go with the stream which carries me along ?   If anything can be done, it must be done not alone but in company with others."

And leaving the most powerful of weapons—thought and its

expression—which move the world, each man employs the weapon of social activity, not noticing that every social activity is based on the very foundations against which he is bound to fight, and that upon entering the social activity which exists in our world every man is obliged, if only in part, to deviate from the truth and to make concessions which destroy the force of the powerful weapon which should assist him in the struggle. It is as though a man, who was given a blade so marvellously keen that it would sever anything, should use its edge for driving in nails.

We all complain of the senseless order of life, which is at variance with our being, and yet we refuse to use the unique and powerful weapon within our hands—the consciousness of truth and its expression; but on the contrary, under the pretext of struggling with evil, we destroy the weapon, and sacrifice it to the exigencies of an imaginary conflict.

One man does not assert the truth which he knows, because he feels himself bound to the people with whom he is engaged; another, because the truth might deprive him of the profitable position by which he maintains his family; a third, because he desires to attain reputation and authority, and then use them in the service of mankind; a fourth, because he does not wish to destroy old sacred traditions; a fifth, because he has no desire to offend people; a sixth, because the expression of the truth would arouse persecution, and disturb the excellent social activity to which he has devoted himself.

One serves as emperor, king, minister, Government official, or soldier, and assures himself and others that the deviation from truth indispensable to his condition is redeemed by the good he does. Another, in the office of a spiritual pastor, does not in the depth of his soul believe all he teaches, but permits the deviation from truth in view of the good he does. A third instructs men by means of literature, and notwithstanding the silence he must observe with regard to the whole truth, in order not to stir up the Government and society against himself, has no doubt as to the good he does. A fourth struggles resolutely with the existing order as revolutionist or anarchist, and is quite assured that the aims he pursues are so beneficial that the neglect of the truth, or even of the falsehood, by silence, indispensable to the success of his activity, does not destroy the utility of his work.

In order that the conditions of a life contrary to the consciousness of humanity should change and be replaced by one which is in accord with it, the outworn public opinion must be superseded by a new and living one.

And in order that the old outworn opinion should yield its place to the new living one, all who are conscious of the new require-ments of existence should openly express them. And yet all those who are conscious of these new requirements, one in the name of one thing, and one in the name of another, not only pass them over in silence, but both by word and deed attest their exact opposites.

Only the truth and its expression can establish that new public opinion which will reform the ancient obsolete and pernicious order of life ; and yet we not only do not express the truth we know, but often even distinctly give expression to what we ourselves regard as false.

If only free men would not rely on that which has no power, and is always fettered—upon external aids; but would trust in that which is always powerful and free—the truth and its expression !

If only men were boldly and clearly to express the truth already manifest to them of the brotherhood of all nations, and the crime of exclusive devotion to one's own people, that defunct, false public opinion would slough off of itself like a dried skin—and upon it depends the power of Governments, and all the evil pro-duced by them—and the new public opinion would stand forth, which is even now but awaiting that dropping off of the old to put forth manifestly and powerfully its demand, and establish new forms of existence in conformity with the consciousness of mankind.

XVIII.

It is sufficient that people should understand that what is enunciated to them as public opinion, and maintained by such complex, energetic, and artificial means, is not public opinion but only the lifeless outcome of what was once public opinion; and what is more important, it is sufficient that they should have faith in themselves, that they should believe that what they are conscious of in the depths of their souls what in everyone is pressing for ex-pression, and is only not expressed because it contradicts the public opinion supposed to exist, is the power which transforms the world, and to express which is the mission of mankind : it is sufficient to believe that truth is not what men talk of, but what is told by his own conscience, that is, by God—and at once the whole artificially maintained public opinion will disappear, and a new one be established in its place.

If people would only speak what they think, and not what they do not think, all the superstitions emanating from patriotism would at once drop away with the cruel feelings and violence founded upon it. The hatred and animosity between nations and peoples, fanned by their Governments, would cease, the extolling of military heroism, that is of murder, would be at an end, and, what is of most importance, respect for authorities, abandonment to them of the fruits of one's labour, and subordination to them would cease, since there is no other reason for them but patriotism.

And if merely this were to take place, that vast mass of feeble people who are controlled by externals would sway at once to the side of the new public opinion, which should reign henceforth in place of the old.

Let the Government keep the schools, Church, Press, its milliards of money and millions of armed men transformed into machines: all this apparently terrible organisation of brute force is as nothing compared to the conciousness of truth, which surges in the soul of one man who knows the power of truth, which is communicated from him to a second and a third, as one candle lights an innumerable quantity of others.

The light needs only to be kindled and, like wax in the face of fire, this organisation, which seems so powerful, will melt, and be consumed.

Only let men understand the vast power which is given them in the word which expresses truth ; only let them refuse to sell their birthright for a mess of pottage ; only let people use their power, and their rulers will not dare, as now, to threaten at their discretion to cast men into a trough of universal slaughter, nor dare before the eyes of a peaceful populace to hold reviews and manœuvres of disciplined murderers ; nor would the Governments dare for their own profit and the advantage of their assistants to arrange and derange custom-house agreements, nor to collect from the people those millions of roubles which they distribute among their assistants, and by the help of which their murders are planned.

And such a transformation is not only possible, but it is as impossible that it should not be accomplished as that a lifeless, decaying tree should not fall, and a younger takes its place.

" Peace I leave with you; my peace I give unto you : not as the world giveth, give I unto you.   Let not your heart be troubled, neither let it be afraid," said Christ.   And this peace is indeed among us, and depends on us for its attainment.

If only the hearts of individuals would not be troubled by the seductions with which they are hourly seduced, nor afraid of those imaginary terrors by which they are intimidated ; if people only knew wherein their chiefest, conquering power consists—a peace which men have always desired, not the peace attainable by diplomatic negotiations, imperial or kingly progresses, dinners, speeches, fortresses, cannon, dynamite, and mélinite, by the exhaustion of the people under taxes, and the abduction from labour of the flower of the population ; but the peace attainable by a voluntary profession of the truth by every man, would long ago have been established.

From *The Daily Chronicle.*

By permission of the Editor.

A REPLY TO CRITICISMS.

[*The following letter was addressed by Count Tolstoy to a Polish journalist, in September of 1895. It is here reproduced, by permission of the Brotherhood Publishing Company, from* THE NEW AGE *of 27th February* 1896.]

A REPLY TO CRITICISMS.

I RECEIVED your letter, and hastened to read your article in *The Northern Messenger*. I am much obliged to you for drawing my attention to this. The article is excellent, and I have learned from it much that was new and joyful to me. I knew about Mitskevitch and Tovianski. But I ascribed their religious direction to the exceptional dispositions of these two individuals. From your article I learn that they are only the forerunners of a Christian movement, so deeply touching in its nobility and sincerity, which has been called forth by patriotism, and which still endures.

My article, "Christianity and Patriotism," evoked very many objections. I received these from philosophers and journalists, Russian, French, German, and Austrian; and now from you. All the objections, yours among them, amount to this: That my condemnation of patriotism is justly applied to bad patriotism, but has no foundation as regards good and useful patriotism. But, as to what constitutes this latter, and how it is distinguishable from bad patriotism, no one has yet troubled to explain.

You say in your letter, that "as well as the militant, inhumane patriotism of strong nations, there is also the opposite patriotism of enslaved nations, who seek only to defend their native faith and language against the enemy." You thus identify good patriotism as the patriotism of the oppressed. But the oppression or the dominance of nations makes no essential difference in what is called patriotism. Fire is always the same burning and dangerous fire, whether it blaze up in a bonfire or flicker in a match.

By "patriotism" is really meant a love for one's own nation above other nations; just as by "egoism" is meant a love for oneself more than for others. It is hard to imagine how such preference for one nation above others can be deemed a good, and therefore a desirable, disposition. If you say that patriotism is more pardonable in the oppressed than in the oppressor, just as a manifestation of egoism is more pardonable in a man who is being strangled than in one who is left in peace, then it is impossible to disagree with you ; nevertheless, patriotism cannot change its nature, whether it is displayed in oppressor or oppressed. This disposition of preference for one nation over all others, like egoism, can in nowise be good.

But not only is patriotism a bad disposition, it is unreasonable in principle.

By patriotism is meant, not only spontaneous, instinctive love for one's own nation, and preference for it above all other nations, but also the belief that such love and preference are good and useful. This belief is especially unreasonable in Christian nations.

It is unreasonable, not only because it runs counter to the first principles of Christ's teachings, but also because Christianity gains, by its own method, everything for which patriotism seeks ; thus making patriotism superfluous, unnecessary, and a hindrance, like a lamp by daylight.

A man who, like Krasinski, believes that "the Church of God is not in this or that place, this or that rite, but in the whole planet, and in all the relations which can exist between individuals and nations "—such a man can no longer be a patriot ; but he will, in the name of Christianity, do all that patriotism can demand of him. For example, patriotism demands of its votary the devotion of his life for the sake of his fellow-countrymen. But Christianity, demanding the same devotion for the good of all men, demands it all the more forcibly and naturally for those of one's own nation.

You write of the terrible acts of violence perpetrated by the savage, stupid, and cruel Russian authorities, directed against the belief and language of the Poles ; and you exhibit these as providing a motive for patriotic action. But I do not see this. To feel indignation at these deeds, and to oppose them with all one's might, it is not necessary to be either a Pole or a patriot ; to be a Christian is enough.

Upon this point I, for instance, who am not a Pole, will yet vie with any Pole in the degree of my abhorrence of, my indignation at, those savage and stupid measures which Russian government officials direct against the Poles. I will vie, also, in the desire to oppose those measures ; and this, not because I care for Catholicism above other religions, or for the Polish language above other tongues, but because I strive to be a Christian. In like manner, for the abolition of such evils, whether in Poland, or Alsace, or Bohemia, we need the spread, not of patriotism, but of true Christianity.

Some may say, " We do not wish to accept Christianity, and we are therefore free to exalt patriotism." But once men have acknowledged Christianity, or at least the perception of human equality and respect for human dignity which flow from Christianity, there is then no longer room for patriotism. What, again, most astonishes me in all this is, that the upholders of the patriotism of the oppressed do not see how harmful patriotism, however perfect and refined they may represent it to be, is to their own particular cause.

Those attacks upon language and religion in Poland, the Baltic provinces, Alsace, Bohemia, upon the Jews in Russia, in every place that such acts of violence occur—in what name have they been, and are they, perpetrated? In none other than the name of that patriotism which you defend.

Ask our savage Russifiers of Poland and the Baltic provinces, ask the persecutors of the Jews, why they act thus. They will tell you it is in defence of their native religion and language; they will tell you that if they do not act thus, their religion and language will suffer—the Russians will be Polonised, Teutonised, Judaised.

Were there no doctrine that patriotism is beneficial, men of the end of the nineteenth century would never be found sunken so low as to determine upon the abominations they at present enact.

Now, learned men (our most savage religious persecutor is an ex-professor) find standing-ground upon patriotism. They know history, they know of all the fruitless horrors of persecution for the sake of language and religion; but, thanks to the doctrine of patriotism, they have a justification.

Patriotism gives them a standing-ground, which Christianity takes from under their feet. Therefore it behoves conquered nations, sufferers from oppression, to destroy patriotism, to destroy its doctrinal foundations, to ridicule it, and not to exalt it.

Defending patriotism, people go on to talk of the individuality of nations, of patriotism aiming to save the individuality of a nation; while the individuality of nations is assumed to be a necessary condition of progress. But, to begin with, who says that such individuality is necessary to progress? This is in no way proved, and we have no right to take such an arbitrary assumption as an axiom. In the next place, even if it be accepted, even then, the way for a nation to assert its individuality is, not to struggle to do so, but, on the contrary, to forget about its individuality, and then to accomplish with all its power that which its people feel themselves most able, and therefore most called upon, to do. Just as an individual will most assert his individuality, not when he pays heed to it, but when, having forgotten about it, he, to the limit of his strength and capacity, does that to which his nature attracts him. So matters would be arranged among a people who, working for their support as a community, must choose different kinds of work and different places. Only let each one follow his strength and capacity in doing what is most necessary to the community, and do this as well as he can, and all will inevitably work differently, with different tools and in different places.

One of the commonest sophisms used in defending immorality consists in wilfully confusing what is with what should be, and, having begun to speak of one thing, substituting another. This very sophism is employed above all in relation to patriotism. It is fact, that to every Pole, the Pole is nearest and dearest ; to the German, the German ; to the Jew, the Jew ; to the Russian, the Russian. It is even true that, through historical causes and bad education, the people of one nation instinctively feel aversion and ill-will to those of another. All this is so ; but to admit it, like admitting the fact that each man loves himself more than he loves others, can in no way prove that it ought so to be. On the contrary, the whole concern of all humanity, and of every individual, lies in suppressing these preferences and aversions, in battling with them, and in deliberately behaving towards other nations and towards individual foreigners, exactly as towards one's own nation and fellow-countrymen. To care for patriotism as an emotion worthy to be cultivated in every man, is wholly superfluous. God, or Nature, has already, without our care, so provided for this feeling that every man has it ; leaving us no cause to trouble about cultivating it in ourselves and others. We must concern ourselves, not about patriotism, but to bring into life that light which is within us ; to change the character of life, and approach it to the ideal which stands before us. That ideal, presented in our time before every man, and illumined with the true light from Christ, has not to do with the resuscitation of Poland, Bohemia, Ireland, Armenia ; has not to do with the preservation of the unity and greatness of Russia, England, Germany, Austria ; but on the contrary, is concerned to destroy this unity and greatness of Russia, England, Germany, Austria, by the destruction of those force-main-tained anti-Christian combinations called States, which stand in the way of all true progress, and occasion the sufferings of oppressed and conquered nations; occasion all those evils from which contemporary humanity suffers. Such destruction is only possible through true enlightenment, resulting in the avowal that we, before being Russians, Poles, Germans, are men, the followers of one teacher, the children of one Father, brothers; and this, the best representatives of the Polish nation understand, as you have so excellently shown in your article. Day by day this is understood by a greater and greater number of people throughout the whole world. So that the days of State violence are already numbered, and the liberation, not only of conquered nations, but of the crushed working-people, is by this time near, if only we ourselves will not delay the time of liberation, by sharing with deed and word in the violent measures of governments. The approval of patriotism of any kind as a good quality, and the incitement of the people to patriotism, is a chief hindrance to the attainment of those ideals which rise before us.

Once more, I thank you very much for your letter, for the excellent article, and for the opportunity you have given me of again reconsidering, verifying, and expressing my ideas on patriotism.

LEO TOLSTOY.

PATRIOTISM, OR PEACE?

[*The following letter, called forth by the dispute about Venezuela between the United States and England, was written by Count Tolstoy to an English correspondent in the early part of the present year (1896), and first appeared in* THE DAILY CHRONICLE *of 17th March.*]

PATRIOTISM, OR PEACE?

You write asking me to state my opinion on the case between the United States and England, "in the cause of Christian consistency and true peace," and you express the hope "that the nations may soon be awakened to the only means of ensuring international peace."

I entertain the same hope; and for this reason. The complication which, in our time, involves the nations: exalting patriotism as they do, educating the young generation in that superstition, and at the same time shirking that inevitable consequence of patriotism,—war: has, it seems to me, reached that last degree at which the very simplest consideration, such as suggests itself to every unbiassed person, may suffice to show to men the extreme contradiction in which they are placed.

Often, when one asks children which they choose of two incompatible but eagerly desired things, they will answer, "Both." "Which do you wish—to go for a drive, or to play at home?" "To go for a drive and to play at home."

Exactly so with the Christian nations, when life itself puts the question to them, "Which do you choose—patriotism or peace?" They answer, "Patriotism and peace." Although to combine patriotism and peace is just as impossible as to go for a drive and to stay at home at one and the same time.

The other day a conflict arose between the United States and England over the frontier of Venezuela. Salisbury did not agree to something; Cleveland wrote a message to the Senate; patriotic, warlike cries were raised on both sides; a panic occurred on 'Change; people lost millions of pounds and dollars; Edison said he was devising machines to kill more men in an hour than were killed by Attila in all his wars; and both nations began to make energetic preparations for war. But, together with these preparations for war, alike in England

and America, various writers, princes, and statesmen began to counsel the governments of both nations to keep from war, insisting that the matter in dispute was not sufficiently serious for war, especially as between two Anglo-Saxon nations, peoples of one language, who ought not to go to war with each other, but rather in amity together domineer over others. Whether because of this, or because all kinds of bishops, clergymen, and ministers prayed and preached over the matter in their churches, or because both sides considered they were not yet ready; for one cause or another, it has turned out there is to be no war this time. And people have calmed down.

But one would have too little penetration not to see that the causes which have thus led to dispute between England and the States still remain the same ; that if the present difficulty is settled without war, yet, inevitably, to-morrow or next day, disputes must arise between England and the States, between England and Germany, England and Russia, England and Turkey, disputes in all possible combinations. Such arise daily ; and one or other of them will surely bring war.

For, if there live side-by-side two armed men, who have from childhood been taught that power, riches, and glory are highest goods, and that to obtain these by arms, to the loss of one's neighbours, is a most praiseworthy thing ; and if, further, there is for these men no moral, religious, or political bound; then is it not clear that they will always seek war, that their normal relations will be warlike, and that, having once caught each other by the throat, they separate again only, as the French proverb has it, *pour mieux sauter*,—they draw back to take a better spring, to rush upon each other with more ferocity?

The egoism of the individual is terrible. But the egoists of private life are not armed ; they do not count it good to prepare, or to use, arms against their competitors; their egoism is controlled by the powers of the State and of public opinion. A private person who should, arms in hand, deprive his neighbour of a cow or an acre of field, would be at once seized by the police, and imprisoned. Moreover, he would be condemned by public opinion; called a thief and a robber. Quite otherwise with states. All are armed. Influence over them there is none ; more than those absurd attempts to catch a bird by sprinkling salt on its tail, such as are the efforts to establish international congresses, which armed states (armed, forsooth, that they may be above taking advice) will clearly never accept. And above all, the public opinion which punishes every violent act of the private individual, praises, exalts as the virtue of patriotism, every appropriation of other people's property made with a view of increasing the power of one's own country.

Open the newspapers on any day you like, and you will always see, every moment, some black spot, a possible cause for war. Now, it is Korea; again, the Pamirs, Africa, Abyssinia, Armenia, Turkey, Venezuela, or the Transvaal. The work of robbery ceases not for an instant; now here, now there, some small war is going on incessantly, like the exchange of shots in the first line; and a great real war may, must, begin at some moment.

If the American desires the greatness and prosperity of the States before all nations, and the Englishman desires the same for his nation, and the Russian, Turk, Dutchman, Abyssinian,, Venezuelan, Boer, Armenian, Pole, Czech, each have a similar desire; if all are convinced that these desires ought not to be concealed and suppressed, but, on the contrary, are something to be proud of, and to be encouraged in oneself and in others; and if one country's greatness and prosperity can only be obtained at the expense of another, or at times of many other countries and nations; then how can war not be?

Obviously, to avoid war, it is necessary, not to preach sermons and pray God for peace, not to adjure the English-speaking nations to live in peace together in order to domineer over other nations, not to make double and triple counter-alliances, not to intermarry princes and princesses, but to destroy the root of war. And that is, the exclusive desire for the well-being of one's own people; it is patriotism. Therefore, to destroy war, destroy patriotism. But to destroy patriotism, it is first necessary to produce conviction that it is an evil; and that is difficult to do. Tell people that war is an evil, and they will laugh; for who does not know it? Tell them that patriotism is an evil, and most will agree; but with a reservation. "Yes," they will say, "wrong patriotism is an evil; but there is another kind, the kind we hold." But just what this good patriotism is, no one explains. If good patriotism consists in inaggressiveness, as many say, still, all patriotism, even if not aggressive, is necessarily retentive; that is, people wish to keep what they have previously conquered. The nation does not exist which was founded without conquest; and conquest can only be retained by the means which achieved it—namely, violence, murder. But if patriotism be not even retentive, it is then the restoring patriotism of conquered and oppressed nations; of Armenians, Poles, Czechs, Irish, and so on. And this patriotism is about the very worst; for it is the most embittered and the most provocative of violence.

Patriotism cannot be good. Why do not people say that egoism may be good? For this might more easily be maintained as to egoism, which is a natural and inborn feeling, than as to patriotism, which is an unnatural feeling, artificially grafted on man.

It will be said, "Patriotism has welded mankind into states, and maintains the unity of states." But men are now united in states ; that work is done ; why now maintain exclusive devotion to one's own state, when this produces terrible evils for all states and nations ? For this same patriotism which welded mankind into states is now destroying those same states. If there were but one patriotism—say of the English only—then it were possible to regard that as conciliatory, or beneficent. But when, as now, there is American patriotism, English, German, French, Russian, all opposed one to another, in this event, patriotism no longer unites, but disunites. To say that patriotism was beneficent, unifying the states, when it flourished in Greece and Rome, and that it is also similarly and equally beneficent now, after eighteen centuries of life under Christianity, is as much as to say that, because ploughing was useful and good for the field before the sowing, it is equally so now, when the crop has come up.

It might, indeed, be well to let patriotism survive, in memory of the benefits it once brought, in the way we preserved ancient monuments, like temples, tombs, and so on. But temples and tombs endure without causing any harm ; while patriotism ceases not to inflict incalculable woes.

Why are Armenians and Turks now agitated, being massacred, becoming like wild beasts? Why are England and Russia, each anxious for its own share of the inheritance from Turkey, waiting upon, and not ending, these butcheries of Armenians ? Why are Abyssinians and Italians being massacred ? Why was a terrible war within an ace of outbreak over Venezuela ; and since, another over the Transvaal ? And the Chino-Japanese war, the Russo-Turkish, the Franco-German ? And the bitterness of conquered nations : Armenians, Poles, Irish ? And the preparations for a war of all nations ? All this is the fruit of patriotism. Seas of blood have been shed over this passion ; and will yet be shed for it, unless people free themselves of this obsolete relic of antiquity.

Several times now I have had occasion to write about patriotism ; about its entire incompatibility, not only with the truly understood teaching of Christ, but with the very lowest demands of morality in a Christian society. Each time my arguments have been met either with silence, or with a lofty suggestion that my ideas, as expressed, are Utopian utterances of mysticism, anarchism, and cosmopolitanism. Often my ideas are summed up, and then, instead of counter-arguments, the remark only is added, that " this is nothing else than cosmopolitanism!" As if this word, cosmopolitanism, had indisputably refuted all my arguments.

Men who are serious, mature, clever, kind, and who—this is the most important matter—stand like a city on a mountain-top; men who by their example involuntarily lead the masses; such men assume that the legitimacy and beneficence of patriotism are so far evident and certain, that it is not worth while answering the frivolous and foolish attacks on the sacred feeling. And the majority of people, misled from childhood, and infected with patriotism, accept this lofty silence as the most convincing argument; and they continue to walk in the darkness of ignorance.

Those who, from their position, can help to free the masses from their sufferings, and do not do so, commit a vast sin.

The most fearful evil in the world is, hypocrisy. Not in vain did Christ, once only, show anger; and that against the hypocrisy of the Pharisees.

But what was Pharisaic hypocrisy compared with the hypocrisy of our own time? In comparison with our hypocrites, those among the Pharisees were the justest of men; and their art of hypocrisy was child's play, beside ours. It cannot be otherwise. All our lives, with their profession of Christianity, of the doctrine of humility and love, lived in an armed robber camp, cannot be other than one unbroken, frightful hypocrisy. It is very convenient to profess a doctrine which has, at one end, Christian holiness and consequent infallibility, and at the other end, the heathen sword and gallows; so that, when it is possible to deceive and impose by holiness, holiness is brought in play, while, when the deceit fails, the sword and gallows are set to work. Such a doctrine is very convenient. But a time comes when the cobweb of lies gives way, and it is no longer possible to keep up both ends; one or other has to go. This is about to happen with the doctrine of patriotism.

Whether people wish it or do not wish it, the question stands clear to mankind, *How can this patriotism, whence come human sufferings incalculable, sufferings both physical and moral, be necessary, and be a virtue?* This question, of compulsion, must be answered.

It is needful, either to show that patriotism is so beneficent that it redeems all those terrible sufferings which it causes to mankind; or else, to acknowledge that patriotism is an evil, which, instead of being grafted upon and suggested to people, should be struggled against with all one's might, to escape from it.

C'est à prendre ou à laisser, as the French say. If patriotism be good, then Christianity, as giving peace, is an idle dream, and the sooner we root it out, the better. But if Christianity really gives peace, and if we really want peace, then patriotism is a survival of barbarism, and it is not only wrong to excite and develop it, as we do now, but it ought to be rooted out by every means, by preaching, persuasion, contempt, ridicule. If Christianity be truth, and we wish to live in peace, then must we more than cease to take pleasure in the power of our country; we must rejoice in the weakening of that power, and help thereto. A Russian should rejoice if Poland, the Baltic Provinces, Finland, Armenia, should be separated, freed, from Russia; so with an Englishman, in regard to Ireland, India, and other possessions; and each should help to this, because, the greater the state, the more wrong and cruel is its patriotism, and the greater is the sum of suffering upon which its power is founded. Therefore, if we really wish to be what we profess to be, we must not only cease our present desire for the growth of our state, but we must desire its decrease, its weakening, and help this forward with all our might. And in this way we must train the rising generation; we must educate them so that, just as now a young man is ashamed to show his rude egoism by eating everything and leaving nothing for others, by pushing the weak out of the way that he may pass himself, by forcibly taking that which another needs: so he may then be equally ashamed of desiring increased power for his own country; and so that, just as it is now considered stupid, foolish, to praise oneself, it shall then be seen to be equally foolish to praise one's own nation, as is now done in divers of the best national histories, pictures, monuments, text-books, articles, verses, sermons, and silly national hymns. It must be understood that, so long as we praise patriotism, and cultivate it in the young, so long will there be armaments to destroy the physical and spiritual life of nations; and wars, vast, awful wars, such as we are preparing for, and into the circle of which we are drawing, debauching them in our patriotism, the new and to be dreaded combatants of the far East.

The Emperor William, one of the most absurd personages of our time,—orator, poet, musician, dramatist and painter, chief of all, patriot, —lately had made a sketch representing all the nations of Europe, standing, with drawn swords, on the sea-shore ; there, under direction of the Archangel Michael, gazing at figures of Buddha and Confucius, seated in the distance. In William's intention, this denotes that the nations of Europe must unite, to oppose the danger moving upon them from the quarter shown. And he is perfectly right ; that is, from his pagan, gross, patriotic point of view, obsolete these eighteen hundred years.

The European nations, forgetful of Christ for the sake of patriotism, have ever more and more excited and incited these peaceful peoples to patriotism ; and now have roused them to such a degree that really, if only Japan and China as completely forget the teaching of Buddha and Confucius as we have forgotten the teaching of Christ, they would soon master the art of killing (soon learned, as Japan has shown) ; and being brave, skilful, strong, and numerous, they would inevitably do with Europe what the European countries are doing with Africa ; unless Europe can oppose to them something stronger than armaments and Edisonian devices. "The disciple is not above his master: but every one that is perfect shall be as his master."

To the question of a petty king, as to how many men, and in what way, he should add to his troops, in order to conquer a southern tribe which refused submission to him, Confucius replied, "Disband all your army, use what you now spend on troops for the education of your people, and for the improvement of agriculture ; and the southern tribe will expel its king, and, without war, submit to thy authority."

Thus taught Confucius, whom we are counselled to fear.

And we, having forgotten the teaching of Christ, having renounced him, wish to subdue nations by violence ; thereby only to prepare for ourselves new enemies, yet more powerful than our present neighbours.

A friend of mine, having seen William's picture, said, "The picture is excellent, only it does not at all signify what is written below. It really shows the Archangel Michael pointing out to all the governments of Europe, represented as brigands hung round with arms, that which is to destroy, annihilate them—namely, the meekness of Buddha and the reasonableness of Confucius." He might have added, "and the humility of Lao-Tse." And indeed we, in our hypocrisy, have so far forgotten Christ, and corroded out of our lives all that is Christian, that the teachings of Buddha and Confucius rise incomparably higher than that bestial patriotism which guides our pseudo-Christian nations.

G

The salvation of Europe, of the whole Christian world, comes not by being girt with swords, like brigands, as in William's picture; not by rushing across seas to kill our brethren: but, oppositely, by casting off that survival of barbarism, patriotism; and having renounced it, by disarming; showing the oriental nations an example, not of savage patriotism and ferocity, but that one of brotherly life which has been taught to us by Christ.

LEO TOLSTOY.

THE WALTER SCOTT PRESS, NEWCASTLE-ON-TYNE.

IBSEN'S PROSE DRAMAS.

EDITED BY WILLIAM ARCHER.

Complete in Five Vols. Crown 8vo, Cloth, Price 3/6 each.
Set of Five Vols., in Case, 17/6; in Half Morocco, in Case, 32/6.

" We seem at last to be shewn men and women as they are ; and at first it is more than we can endure. . . . All Ibsen's characters speak and act as if they were hypnotised, and under their creator's imperious demand to reveal themselves. There never was such a mirror held up to nature before: it is too terrible. . . . Yet we must return to Ibsen, with his remorseless surgery, his remorseless electric-light, until we, too, have grown strong and learned to face the naked—if necessary, the flayed and bleeding—reality."—SPEAKER (London).

VOL. I. "A DOLL'S HOUSE," "THE LEAGUE OF YOUTH," and "THE PILLARS OF SOCIETY." With Portrait of the Author, and Biographical Introduction by WILLIAM ARCHER.

VOL. II. "GHOSTS," "AN ENEMY OF THE PEOPLE," and "THE WILD DUCK." With an Introductory Note.

VOL. III. "LADY INGER OF ÖSTRÅT," "THE VIKINGS AT HELGELAND," "THE PRETENDERS." With an Introductory Note and Portrait of Ibsen.

VOL. IV. "EMPEROR AND GALILEAN." With an Introductory Note by WILLIAM ARCHER.

VOL. V. "ROSMERSHOLM," "THE LADY FROM THE SEA," "HEDDA GABLER." Translated by WILLIAM ARCHER. With an Introductory Note.

The sequence of the plays *in each volume* is chronological ; the complete set of volumes comprising the dramas thus presents them in chronological order.

"The art of prose translation does not perhaps enjoy a very high literary status in England, but we have no hesitation in numbering the present version of Ibsen, so far as it has gone (Vols. I. and II.), among the very best achievements, in that kind, of our generation."—*Academy*.

"We have seldom, if ever, met with a translation so absolutely idiomatic."—*Glasgow Herald*.

London : WALTER SCOTT, LIMITED, Paternoster Square.

GREAT WRITERS.

A NEW SERIES OF CRITICAL BIOGRAPHIES.

Edited by ERIC ROBERTSON and FRANK T. MARZIALS.

A Complete Bibliography to each Volume, by J. P. ANDERSON,
British Museum, London.

Cloth, Uncut Edges, Gilt Top. Price 1/6.

VOLUMES ALREADY ISSUED—

LIFE OF LONGFELLOW.	By Professor Eric S. Robertson.
LIFE OF COLERIDGE.	By Hall Caine.
LIFE OF DICKENS.	By Frank T. Marzials.
LIFE OF DANTE GABRIEL ROSSETTI.	By J. Knight.
LIFE OF SAMUEL JOHNSON.	By Colonel F. Grant.
LIFE OF DARWIN.	By G. T. Bettany.
LIFE OF CHARLOTTE BRONTË.	By A. Birrell.
LIFE OF THOMAS CARLYLE.	By R. Garnett, LL.D.
LIFE OF ADAM SMITH.	By R. B. Haldane, M.P.
LIFE OF KEATS.	By W. M. Rossetti.
LIFE OF SHELLEY.	By William Sharp.
LIFE OF SMOLLETT.	By David Hannay.
LIFE OF GOLDSMITH.	By Austin Dobson.
LIFE OF SCOTT.	By Professor Yonge.
LIFE OF BURNS.	By Professor Blackie.
LIFE OF VICTOR HUGO.	By Frank T. Marzials.
LIFE OF EMERSON.	By Richard Garnett, LL.D.
LIFE OF GOETHE.	By James Sime.
LIFE OF CONGREVE.	By Edmund Gosse.
LIFE OF BUNYAN.	By Canon Venables.
LIFE OF CRABBE.	By T. E. Kebbel.
LIFE OF HEINE.	By William Sharp.
LIFE OF MILL.	By W. L. Courtney.
LIFE OF SCHILLER.	By Henry W. Nevinson.
LIFE OF CAPTAIN MARRYAT.	By David Hannay.
LIFE OF LESSING.	By T. W. Rolleston.
LIFE OF MILTON.	By R. Garnett, LL.D.
LIFE OF BALZAC.	By Frederick Wedmore.
LIFE OF GEORGE ELIOT.	By Oscar Browning.
LIFE OF JANE AUSTEN.	By Goldwin Smith.
LIFE OF BROWNING.	By William Sharp.
LIFE OF BYRON.	By Hon. Roden Noel.
LIFE OF HAWTHORNE.	By Moncure D. Conway.
LIFE OF SCHOPENHAUER.	By Professor Wallace.
LIFE OF SHERIDAN.	By Lloyd Sanders.
LIFE OF THACKERAY.	By Herman Merivale and Frank T. Marzials.
LIFE OF CERVANTES.	By H. E. Watts.
LIFE OF VOLTAIRE.	By Francis Espinasse.
LIFE OF LEIGH HUNT.	By Cosmo Monkhouse.
LIFE OF WHITTIER.	By W. J. Linton.
LIFE OF RENAN.	By Francis Espinasse.
LIFE OF THOREAU.	By H. S. Salt.

LIBRARY EDITION OF "GREAT WRITERS," Demy 8vo, 2s. 6d.

London : WALTER SCOTT, LIMITED, Paternoster Square.

THE SCOTT LIBRARY.

Cloth, Uncut Edges, Gilt Top.   Price 1s. 6d. per Volume.

VOLUMES ALREADY ISSUED—

1 ROMANCE OF KING ARTHUR.
2 THOREAU'S WALDEN.
3 THOREAU'S "WEEK."
4 THOREAU'S ESSAYS.
5 ENGLISH OPIUM-EATER.
6 LANDOR'S CONVERSATIONS.
7 PLUTARCH'S LIVES.
8 RELIGIO MEDICI, &c.
9 SHELLEY'S LETTERS.
10 PROSE WRITINGS OF SWIFT.
11 MY STUDY WINDOWS.
12 THE ENGLISH POETS.
13 THE BIGLOW PAPERS.
14 GREAT ENGLISH PAINTERS.
15 LORD BYRON'S LETTERS.
16 ESSAYS BY LEIGH HUNT.
17 LONGFELLOW'S PROSE.
18 GREAT MUSICAL COMPOSERS.
19 MARCUS AURELIUS.
20 TEACHING OF EPICTETUS.
21 SENECA'S MORALS.
22 SPECIMEN DAYS IN AMERICA.
23 DEMOCRATIC VISTAS.
24 WHITE'S SELBORNE.
25 DEFOE'S SINGLETON.
26 MAZZINI'S ESSAYS.
27 PROSE WRITINGS OF HEINE.
28 REYNOLDS' DISCOURSES.
29 PAPERS OF STEELE AND ADDISON.
30 BURNS'S LETTERS.
31 VOLSUNGA SAGA.
32 SARTOR RESARTUS.
33 WRITINGS OF EMERSON.
34 LIFE OF LORD HERBERT.
35 ENGLISH PROSE.
36 IBSEN'S PILLARS OF SOCIETY.
37 IRISH FAIRY AND FOLK TALES.
38 ESSAYS OF DR. JOHNSON.
39 ESSAYS OF WILLIAM HAZLITT.
40 LANDOR'S PENTAMERON, &c.
41 POE'S TALES AND ESSAYS.
42 VICAR OF WAKEFIELD.
43 POLITICAL ORATIONS.
44 AUTOCRAT OF THE BREAK-FAST-TABLE.
45 POET AT THE BREAKFAST-TABLE.
46 PROFESSOR AT THE BREAK-FAST-TABLE.
47 CHESTERFIELD'S LETTERS.
48 STORIES FROM CARLETON.

49 JANE EYRE.
50 ELIZABETHAN ENGLAND.
51 WRITINGS OF THOMAS DAVIS
52 SPENCE'S ANECDOTES.
53 MORE'S UTOPIA.
54 SADI'S GULISTAN.
55 ENGLISH FAIRY TALES.
56 NORTHERN STUDIES.
57 FAMOUS REVIEWS.
58 ARISTOTLE'S ETHICS.
59 PERICLES AND ASPASIA.
60 ANNALS OF TACITUS.
61 ESSAYS OF ELIA.
62 BALZAC.
63 DE MUSSET'S COMEDIES.
64 CORAL REEFS.
65 SHERIDAN'S PLAYS.
66 OUR VILLAGE.
67 MASTER HUMPHREY'S CLOCK
68 TALES FROM WONDERLAND.
69 JERROLD'S ESSAYS.
70 THE RIGHTS OF WOMAN.
71 "THE ATHENIAN ORACLE."
72 ESSAYS OF SAINTE-BEUVE.
73 SELECTIONS FROM PLATO.
74 HEINE'S TRAVEL SKETCHES.
75 MAID OF ORLEANS.
76 SYDNEY SMITH.
77 THE NEW SPIRIT.
78 MALORY'S BOOK OF MAR-VELLOUS ADVENTURES.
79 HELPS' ESSAYS & APHORISMS.
80 ESSAYS OF MONTAIGNE.
81 THACKERAY'S BARRY LYNDON.
82 SCHILLER'S WILLIAM TELL.
83 CARLYLE'S GERMAN ESSAYS.
84 LAMB'S ESSAYS.
85 WORDSWORTH'S PROSE.
86 LEOPARDI'S DIALOGUES.
87 THE INSPECTOR-GENERAL.
88 BACON'S ESSAYS.
89 PROSE OF MILTON.
90 PLATO'S REPUBLIC.
91 PASSAGES FROM FROISSART.
92 PROSE OF COLERIDGE.
93 HEINE IN ART AND LETTERS.
94 ESSAYS OF DE QUINCEY.
95 VASARI'S LIVES OF ITALIAN PAINTERS.
96 LESSING'S LAOCOON.
97 PLAYS OF MAETERLINCK.
98 WALTON'S COMPLETE ANGLER.
99 LESSING'S NATHAN THE WISE.

May be had in the following Bindings:—Cloth, uncut edges, gilt top, 1s. 6d.; Half-Morocco, gilt top, antique; Red Roan, gilt edges, etc.

London : WALTER SCOTT, LIMITED, Paternoster Square.

THE CANTERBURY POETS.

EDITED BY WILLIAM SHARP. IN 1/- MONTHLY VOLUMES.

Cloth, Cut and Uncut Edges, 1s.; Red Roan, Gilt Edges, 2s. 6d.;
Pad. Morocco, Gilt Edges, 5s.

A SUPERIOR EDITION BOUND IN ART LINEN, WITH PHOTOGRAVURE FRONTISPIECE. PRICE 2s.

1 CHRISTIAN YEAR
2 COLERIDGE
3 LONGFELLOW
4 CAMPBELL
5 SHELLEY
6 WORDSWORTH
7 BLAKE
8 WHITTIER
9 POE
10 CHATTERTON
11 BURNS. Songs
12 BURNS. Poems
13 MARLOWE
14 KEATS
15 HERBERT
16 HUGO
17 COWPER
18 SHAKESPEARE'S POEMS, etc.
19 EMERSON
20 SONNETS OF THIS CENTURY
21 WHITMAN
22 SCOTT. Lady of the Lake, etc.
23 SCOTT. Marmion, etc.
24 PRAED
25 HOGG
26 GOLDSMITH
27 LOVE LETTERS, etc.
28 SPENSER
29 CHILDREN OF THE POETS
30 JONSON
31 BYRON. Miscellaneous.
32 BYRON. Don Juan.
33 THE SONNETS OF EUROPE
34 RAMSAY
35 DOBELL
36 POPE
37 HEINE
38 BEAUMONT & FLETCHER
39 BOWLES, LAMB, etc.
40 SEA MUSIC
41 EARLY ENGLISH POETRY
42 HERRICK
43 BALLADES AND RONDEAUS
44 IRISH MINSTRELSY
45 MILTON'S PARADISE LOST
46 JACOBITE BALLADS
47 DAYS OF THE YEAR
48 AUSTRALIAN BALLADS
49 MOORE
50 BORDER BALLADS
51 SONG-TIDE
52 ODES OF HORACE
53 OSSIAN
54 FAIRY MUSIC
55 SOUTHEY
56 CHAUCER
57 GOLDEN TREASURY
58 POEMS OF WILD LIFE
59 PARADISE REGAINED
60 CRABBE
61 DORA GREENWELL
62 FAUST
63 AMERICAN SONNETS
64 LANDOR'S POEMS
65 GREEK ANTHOLOGY
66 HUNT AND HOOD
67 HUMOROUS POEMS
68 LYTTON'S PLAYS
69 GREAT ODES
70 MEREDITH'S POEMS
71 IMITATION OF CHRIST
72 UNCLE TOBY BIRTHDAY BK
73 PAINTER-POETS
74 WOMEN POETS
75 LOVE LYRICS
76 AMERICAN HUMOROUS VERSE.
77 MINOR SCOTCH LYRICS
78 CAVALIER LYRISTS
79 GERMAN BALLADS
80 SONGS OF BERANGER
81 RODEN NOEL'S POEMS
82 SONGS OF FREEDOM
83 CANADIAN POEMS
84 CONTEMPORARY SCOTTISH VERSE
85 POEMS OF NATURE
86 CRADLE SONGS.
87 BALLADS OF SPORT.
88 MATTHEW ARNOLD.

London: WALTER SCOTT, LIMITED, Paternoster Square.

NEW EDITION IN NEW BINDING.

In the new edition there are added about forty reproductions in fac-simile of autographs of distinguished singers and instrumentalists, including Sarasate, Joachim, Sir Charles Hallé, Stavenhagen, Henschel, Trebelli, Miss Macintyre, Jean Gérardy, etc.

Quarto, cloth elegant, gilt edges, emblematic design on cover, 6s.
May also be had in a variety of Fancy Bindings.

THE
MUSIC OF THE POETS:
A MUSICIANS' BIRTHDAY BOOK.

EDITED BY ELEONORE D'ESTERRE KEELING.

This is a unique Birthday Book. Against each date are given the names of musicians whose birthday it is, together with a verse-quotation appropriate to the character of their different compositions or performances. A special feature of the book consists in the reproduction in fac-simile of autographs, and autographic music, of living composers. The selections of verse (from before Chaucer to the present time) have been made with admirable critical insight. English verse is rich in utterances of the poets about music, and merely as a volume of poetry about music this book makes a charming anthology. Three sonnets by Mr. Theodore Watts, on the "Fausts" of Berlioz, Schumann, and Gounod, have been written specially for this volume. It is illustrated with designs of various musical instruments, etc.; autographs of Rubenstein, Dvořák, Greig, Mackenzie, Villiers Stanford, etc., etc.

"To musical amateurs this will certainly prove the most attractive birthday book ever published."—*Manchester Guardian.*

LONDON: WALTER SCOTT, LIMITED, PATERNOSTER SQUARE.